# My Summer with MOLLY

### The Journal of a
### Second Generation Father

BY THE SAME AUTHOR

Shadow of a Continent

California Quake

Long Beach: Fortune's Harbor
(Co-Authored with Patricia Kalayjian)

The Complete Works of Marcus Uteris

# My Summer with MOLLY

## The Journal of a Second Generation Father

Larry L. Meyer
Illustrations by Elin Waite

SAU MAGALE LIBRARY

Calafia Press

Huntington Beach, CA.

Copyright 1989 by Calafia Press

All Rights Reserved. No part of this book may be reproduced in any form or by any mechanical means without written permission of the publisher.

First Edition

Printed in the United States of America

Library of Congress Cataloging-in-Publication Data

Meyer, Larry L., 1933-
  My summer with Molly: the journal of a second generation father/ Larry L. Meyer; illustrations by Elin Waite. — 1st ed.

1. Meyer, Larry L., 1933- —Diaries. 2. Fathers—United States—Diaries. 3. Middle aged men—United States—Diaries. 4. Fathers and daughters—United States. I. Title.
HQ756.M49 1989
306.8'742'0924—dc19                                                          89-840
                                                                              CIP

ISBN 0-942273-04-4 (alk. paper): $16.95

For Jeannette Elizabeth Stoebe
And All the Other Great Mothers,
Living or Dead

# May 12     *Labor Day*

"I think it's started." Timarie's voice sounds of cool grim excitement over the phone.

My watch reads 3:07 p.m., Monday, May 12. "Are you sure?" The baby girl we had taken such elaborate measures to conceive, so she would be born the week I gave final exams, wasn't due for ten days. "Remember, the first one's usually late," I remind her.

"When I saw Dr. Keel this morning, he said I was dilated to one centimeter. Now the pains are five minutes or less apart. They've been that way for about 40 minutes." Her voice is calm, but an underlying tension lets me know that the one thing I have ever seen my 26-year-old wife show any real apprehension over, labor, is close at hand.

"Hold on, I'll be right there."

Driving home from the university calls up memories more than 19 years old. Then, with my first wife, who was dilated to five centimeters and expecting twins, I drove the ten miles to the hospital on legs that handled the accelerator and brake pedals like strands of cooked spaghetti; 40 minutes after I safely delivered her to the emergency room, she was safely delivered of two boys, to go with the 15-month-old boy at home. I have matured some since then. My legs feel numb but firm this time.

Timarie is just finishing the packing when I get home. Two suitcases holding enough for a migration to Alaska: clothes and underclothes, nightgown, nursing bra, make-up, unguents, potions, backup toothbrushes, cassette tapes of Mozart, Dvorak, Vivaldi, a baby outfit in pink, a baby outfit in blue (why? had she lost her faith?), receiving blankets, a sock stuffed with two tennis balls....

"What are the tennis balls for?"

"You don't remember?" The look is accusatory.

"Should I?" Has she scheduled a match with the labor nurse?

"You use them as a back massager. Don't you remember them telling us that in class?"

"Forgot."

That wasn't the only thing I'd forgotten from our eight Wednesday-night lessons in Prepared Childbirth Class. I should have just taken a written final and hoped for a "Gentleman's C."

Into Timarie's creaky '69 Cougar I jam it all, including an infant's car seat that rests eerily empty on the rear upholstery, and at 4:20 p.m. we are on our way to Humana Hospital, a mere three miles away and chosen in large part for its nearness. I experience some angina, but the legs remain sound, thick, uncooked linguine.

I feel strangely detached, disassociated, right through the admitting process and down to the labor room where things go swimmingly. Timarie's contractions aren't painful. A piece of cake so far, though I'm beginning to wish I'd taken notes during those eight weeks of prenatal classes.

Timarie's mother, Margaret, who has had nine children herself and never seen a one of them actually born, arrives at 5:55 p.m.; she has come to behold the miracle with me, and to help me help Tim through our attempt at modified-Lamaze childbirth.

At 7:05 p.m. Dr. William Keel, Timarie's obstetrician, appears. He examines her and informs us she's dilated to three centimeters and is 70 percent effaced, numbers that I interpret as indications labor is progressing nicely. Ten, as I recall, is our goal, when the cervix is dilated to its ten-centimeter or four-inches-open max; the effacement percentage I'm less sure about, but I think it has to do with the thinning and retreating of the cervix, which separates the unborn child from the birth-canal exit. I need some crib notes.

Timarie begins to curse the pain, her mood darkening intermittently. I dutifully wait with her another fitful hour, then start feeling abdominal pains of my own. Yep, it's past my dinner time, but, I'm informed by the floor nurse, it's just past 8:00 p.m. and the hospital cafeteria has closed. Meaning I, the official coach, would have to go out for dinner and abandon my suffering young wife. Hunger grapples with guilt, gains a clear advantage.

"Why don't you just go out and get something to eat?" Timarie asks, rather curtly, I think, but sensitive to my needs. Well, OK then. Progress has slowed...looks like we're in for the long haul. And my pass has been signed by the captain herself. Besides, Margaret has already eaten, so Timarie won't be left alone.

Molly's Eve, as I've dubbed it, has pinks in the palms, and a pinky nail of a moon arcing down on the clear purple air—yet another original evening for which California is rightly famous. Molly Margaret is the musical name chosen for our little girl. I have caught a lot of flak from friends for referring to the unborn child as a female, particularly since the fourth-month sonogram proved inconclusive.

Call it arrogance, if you will. I call it faith. Better, faith in science. Timarie bought a book, *How To Choose the Sex of Your Baby*, and we read and reread it, and Tim kept temperature charts to track ovulation for many months before conception. As an old pony player, I'm giving 9 to 1 it's a girl child.

When I go into a fancy burger joint, my guilt that Timarie, hooked up to an I.V., is denied the taste of the sandwich and Heineken and pleasantly overcooked French fries openly adds to my gustatory pleasure. I take my time, not rushing the meal, sensing that some trial awaits me back at the hospital.

I'm right. Timarie's labor is not to be an easy one. The pain is now fierce and the contractions irregular; the nurse says she's dilated to two centimeters, which is regress, as I reckon it. Or else somebody is wrong.

More important, Tim's been told she can't use the Alternate Birthing Center (or ABC room), as we'd planned and counted on, because the hospital is a nurse short and one expectant mother is in a serious way with toxemia. Timarie is more than angry. She's outraged. So between labor pains she calls in the entire nursing staff for a one-by-one read-out that includes a denunciation of the hospital for fraud and false advertising.

The floor nurse is patiently unyielding, and points out that A) no guarantees of use of the ABC room were made and, if one consulted the fine print, B) Timarie's complicated labor rules out the use of the ABC room anyway.

You couldn't argue the logic, but my wife did, vehemently, as I stood mutely by, a stranger in a strange land of potions and tubes and cords and the all-consuming presence of the fetal monitor, a contraption that straps around the bulging belly and connects electrically to a bedside machine. None of the staff is converted.

Tim's pain pains me, helpless as I am to relieve it. My words of encouragement, memorized from four Wednesday night rehearsals with pillows on the floor of the prenatal classroom, sound just that—rehearsed...phony. To me. So I take refuge in studious observation of the fetal monitor, which simultaneously displays on moving chart paper the nasty spikes of Timarie's labor pains—the less common bi-pinnacled and tri-pinnacled variety—and the unborn child's steady heartbeat.

I study the slightly wavy ink trace on the graph for three to five minutes, watching for the abrupt movement of the pen arm into the higher intensity range.

"You're having a contraction," I tell Timarie.

She moans and writhes. I'm right.

Four minutes later the pen arm leaps again. "Here comes another one!"

She's wincing. And, it appears, glaring at me through that wince. Am I telling her something she already knows? Hey! I'm not a healer. I'm just a coach. Doing my job. And I'm new to it. Why pick on me?

At precisely 10:30 p.m. someone—something—accidentally pulls the cord to the monitor, leaving a straight line trace of no heartbeat or contractions on the recorder paper. Panic stuns me. I am too intimidated by my ignorance to scream and order the nurses to revive my unborn child in utero. Fortunately, an ultra-nice labor nurse named Lisa, who has just come on duty and by great good luck was our instructor in prenatal classes, reads my face and the monitor, spots my problem, and replugs the machine. Molly lives!

But nothing else changes. The labor drags on toward midnight without any apparent progress. So between the four-minute-apart double-spiked and triple-spiked pangs we all peek up at that omnipresent other machine, the greatest friend of hospitals and their guests: the boob-tube. As with all American hospitals I've been in, the mercy of television is never out of sight (except, I suppose, in surgery). And who's to argue against this modern morphine, which turns our attention away from the hurtful reality of now, from the true and terrible intimacies fired in pain? Who needs it? Who wants them?

So as Timarie yelps and twists, Margaret and I anesthetize ourselves with the fatuousness of a *Hawaii 5-0* rerun, the academic value of Ted Koppel's earnest delving into the SDI, the smooth opiate of Johnny's amiable glibness with a forgettable guest.

Through it all—the tension, the anticipation, the distractions—I wonder. . . .Is this any place for a 53-year-old father of three grown sons, newly embarked on a second marriage to a former student who is pregnant with his child, to be?

# May 13  *Birth*

At midnight a decision is made. Agreed upon, really, by the medical staff. Since nothing is going to happen soon (dilation has shrunk to a new observer's finger from two to one-and-a-half centimeters, and the strong labor pains continue in their erratic and unpromising way), the disheartened Timarie is given a pill to ease the pain and build her strength with a short night's sleep; I will retire to the Father's Lounge for some much-needed shut-eye. Margaret, fueled by multiple cups of coffee and anxiety, will stand guard in the labor room and warn us of any changes in nature's plan.

I get more sleep than I do rest, and I don't get too much of either, which is not necessarily attributable to being worried. At six-feet four inches, and with a recent history of back trouble, I simply don't fit into love seats; and the sad fact that I didn't realize until it was much too late—about 5:00 a.m. I think—that the chair I finally collapse into has a reclining capability doesn't help a bit.

At 6:34 a.m. I stagger back to my coaching duties, which, as Timarie comes out from under the previous night's Nisentil (she contemptuously refers to it as "niceuntil," as she heard it described by other mothers for its virtue of granting sleep only until the next contraction strikes), seem to me unappreciated. Yes, the contractions are continuing at the previous evening's ferocity. I see more than a hint of tears in Timarie's eyes for the first time during labor.

"Let's try our Tee-breathing," I suggest in semi-desperation. Her glare informs me I've goofed again. Not only am I premature with this late-in-labor technique, as it turns out, but even in our practice sessions she complained that I never "paced" her properly, that she still had to do all the rhythmic breathing on her own. Rhythm, not ripeness (which I have in abundance), is all, apparently.

"You blew it," she barely hisses between contractions. Clearly, my coaching job is in jeopardy. (I have read that I might face abuse, and I know that I must be brave. Why, Chuck Cottier was fired as manager of the Seattle Mariners the previous Friday! So I'm on the chopping block as my wife's coach this Tuesday. Hey, that's baseball.)

Timarie gets a shot. "Demerol for breakfast please," she sings out to the nurse in forced good humor. I like her spirit. I wish she liked mine.

Eileen, one of Timarie's five sisters, arrives at 7:45 a.m. to help me out. I take a step back, in deference to experience, and let the ordeal of labor, which seems to be taking a lot longer than advertised, torture Timarie further.

By 8:40 a.m. I'm enjoying a resurgence of confidence. I crowd closer to the bed as a wicked pain shows itself on the graph paper. "You're looking good...you're doing fine."

"Please don't breathe in my face."

I hold my ground. "It won't be long now."

The look I get drips with disgust. My words apparently have as much credibility as if I had told her storks deliver babies. I can't figure it. Here I'm holding up my half of the bargain surprisingly well, under increasingly difficult circumstances, and yet with each passing hour of marathon labor I'm getting looks of greater displeasure...indeed, they almost border on contempt.

"Look at the butterflies on the wall," I tell Tim. I'm trying to distract her from her pain by having her concentrate on some small plastic objects as she breathes, the way I remember being taught in prenatal class.

Her glare of wordless rage tells me I've made another major boo-boo.

"Look at the *bows*," Eileen corrects me.

It turns out they are not butterflies at all, but bow-shaped barrettes that Eileen has removed from Tim's hair and fixed to the wall, barrettes which little old unobserving me didn't notice or recognize...even when she was wearing them. I get the feeling I'm about to be relieved of my duties.

At 8:44 Lisa enters and, per Dr. Keel's phoned orders, adds something to the I.V. What is it? Pitocin...some kind of synthetic hormone for females I vaguely recall as having semi-magical properties at times like these.

At 9:00 a.m. sharp the anesthesiologist arrives to give Timarie an epidural—a blend of painkillers that is to be shot into the epidural cavity (not into the spinal fluid); a catheter will keep the juice coming intermittently. We are finally getting somewhere.

The anesthesiologist, a very kindly man in his early sixties, asks for my assistance. My job is to hold Timarie still from the front while he injects from the rear the ultimate cocktail-in-a-needle; it's the modern compromise between the total-thud knockout of Margaret's ether and being among nature's overfolks who learn to live and smile through pain by dint of their spiritual superiority—candidates all for natural dentistry. How did our species ever survive before anesthetics?

When I release Timarie from my hold she looks arrows at me. Why? What now? I follow the direction of her eyes, which "point" to a row of pens in the breast pocket of my shirt. Uuh!... seems I had crushed her against them.

The drug kicks in with astonishing suddenness.

"I'm actually a very pleasant person, believe it or not," Timarie says. I think she's addressing me, but the words are actually for the anesthesiologist. "When I'm not in labor."

I can vouch for that. But right now I'm going to keep it to myself.

To my wife's great relief, the second nurse, Sylvia, brings her a banana Popsicle to suck on—her first liquid in 18 hours. Then, in a matter of minutes, the expectant mother falls asleep.

The anesthesiologist leaves. So do the nurses for a time. Eileen has already left. Margaret has stepped out for a cigarette. I'm left alone with my thoughts, which are turning sharply down. Against my wishes, I find myself dragged into depression and self-accusation; neither is ever very far away, no matter where I am or what I'm doing. How dare a spent old rogue like me even think of fathering another child? What arrogance! What self-indulgence! And look what it's come to! All this suffering... for what? A child I've still not seen?

Schopenhauer's mordant capsule of pessimism pops into my mind: "What crime did this child commit that it should have been born?" There follow a parade of deformities she wears, courtesy of my possibly defective genes or aging cytoplasm—or worse, some undetected and undiagnosed social disease picked up in a reckless youth. Cycloptic... missing ears... massive lesions on the torso... the empty face and gaze of idiocy.

At 2:15 p.m. Dr. Keel, who's been called by the nurses, comes to Timarie's bedside. Just in time, I'm hoping. He is all calm unconcern. But efficient. Timarie has dilated to nine-plus and is 90 percent effaced. The doctor breaks the water bag to help accelerate the birthing process; we have turned into the homestretch of this twenty-five hour marathon labor.

Labor nurse Lisa gives Timarie more pitocin. Her labor pains suddenly quicken; the cries intensify. Now things really start happening. At 2:47 the doctor attaches the fetal monitor directly to the unborn baby's head via a small device that actually is secured to the scalp by a spring; a catheter is also inserted into the vagina to tap the urine and relieve the bladder's pressure on the baby's head.

The doctor has found the baby to be slightly meconium, meaning it has had a bowel movement in utero; the chance that the greenish fecal matter might invade the infant's about-to-function lungs makes delays inadvisable.

The labor pains mount, come faster, their still-double and triple spikes registering on the print-out against background cries. Timarie's time has come, the doctor decides. Get thee to delivery.

Off we go, the movable bed and expectant mother surrounded by the delivery team and its portable instruments and life-monitoring systems, the short distance down the maternity ward hall.

My time has come, too. Delivery has been my chief source of worry since I decided to be a modern father and see what birth is all about. I've never been much for gore. During my five years in the Air Force I witnessed three plane crashes, and in each one I was the guy with eyes quickly averted to see as little of the carnage as I could. Now my loved one is on the delivery table. Will I disgrace myself? Faint? And if I do, who will coach? More important, who will take the birth pictures, the vital mission Timarie has entrusted to me? Margaret, at my side as we follow the gurney into a large chamber that resembles a roomy-but-clean kitchen, got off lucky with the tape-recorder duty.

I surprise myself. In the delivery room I suddenly develop the sangfroid of a brain surgeon. Well, maybe a brain surgeon's assistant's assistant. Between snapping photos, I wipe perspiration from Timarie's forehead as Dr. Keel, Nurse Lisa and Nurse Sylvia at the foot of the table coax my young wife through the bearing down and pushing out. I join them in their encouraging "push hard" and "keep it coming" and "give it all you've got" cries, until a little patch of dark matted fuzz is visible in the vaginal opening. It takes me a few seconds to realize this is the baby's head and not some inner tissue of the mother being forced out to where it doesn't belong.

My new-found courage has limits...or at least I fear it will. As the doctor does the episiotomy with surgical scissors, I turn my eyes at the first spurt of red. I can't risk collapsing in the clutch, can I? Timarie, who has been given a local anesthetic and probably wouldn't have felt anything anyway over the greater masking labor pain, doesn't react at all. (After the baby emerges, while the local still has its deadening effect, the cut will be sewn up, we've been told, to heal completely at some vague future time.)

And then—as if to make up for all the painful delay—time-in-a-rush telescopes as the birth begins...the disproportionately large head confronting first the outer world as Timarie orders through a cry of ecstatic pain, "Pictures!"

"We've plenty of time for pictures," the doctor says in an authoritarian voice, though I've been cooly clicking off shots through the shifting screen posed by the doctor and two nurses. "Let's get the kid out."

And that he does, his hands pulling and easing the new life into the bright light, then briskly going to a suction pump to suck out mucous from the newly operational respiratory system, while I stand stilled in awe.

"Do I have a little squirmer?" Timarie asks in the same ecstatic cry.

I crane my neck, seeing first the child, then the thick, multi-colored elongated umbilical cord I mistake for a split-second as male genitalia on a gargantuan scale. At 3:26 p.m. all is clear...except for the placenta still inside.

"We have a little Molly Margaret," I burble reassuringly.

"We do? We do? Ooooohhhh." Her moan carries the same thrill, against Molly's first beautifully loud and indignant cries at being.

The new mother is suddenly briefly businesslike. "How does she look?"

"She's fine," the doctor immediately reassures her, inured to such inquiries into the baby's physical condition.

"She's a redhead," I add, stunned by this wholly unanticipated roll of the genetic dice.

"She iiiis?!" The voice of teary ecstasy remains.

Molly continues her angry wails as the doctor cuts and clamps the cord; the nurses wipe my little girl off and wrap her in a towel-like blanket. My mind is clearer than I can remember it ever being. My eyes are seeing and recording beyond what I photograph: the baby's head molded at birth into a loaf shape, like the head of a Yoruba tribeswoman...the strange purple spectacle of the afterbirth...the red trickle-down from Timarie's episiotomy...the little red birthmark on the back of Molly's left thigh...the small patch of blood on her crown where the fetal monitor was screwed in.

"Will you put her on me?" Timarie begs. Dr. Keel sets the squawling infant on her mother's chest. "Hello, my little angel girl!" Molly's cries magically subside. "You've got your father's nose already! Larry, touch the little angel girl" is the plaintive command.

I do, the skin softer than putty. I notice her hands and feet are pale.

"Is that vernix?" I ask Sylvia, having read about the waxy substance that often covers newborns.

"No, just a lack of circulation," the nurse answers. "It takes a while for the blood to get going."

The labor pain gone, what she's worked so long and hard to deliver delivered, Timarie becomes suddenly talkative and begins reviewing the highlights of the ordeal.

"Want to do it again?" the doctor asks.

"Get funny!"

The banter, the clean up, and Tim's sewing up continues, but I leave the delivery room for more exhilarating work. The time has come for Molly to be officially measured and weighed into the world, and I, lucky guy under this new plan for parenting, get to accompany her and a nurse into the nursery. I even get to fondle her in her little plastic crib-cradle between measurings. Seven pounds, 11 ounces is where the scale stops; 19-and-a-half inches long is the tale of the tape.

The nurse affixes the identifying plastic band around a tiny ankle, telling the world that this little miracle is Molly Margaret Meyer. As I've both read and been told, most infants are most alert the hour after they are born. Anxious to meet Mom and Dad? Who's to say?

Molly is sure alert. When I put my face close to hers (and under this new plan there's no shooing Dad off because he might be carrying germs), she appears to study me, the first human face she's looked into very long. What an honor! Her limbs are long and fair, her eyes are big and a violet-blue. . .I hope they stay that way.

A little more than an hour after birth, Mom and Molly and Dad are reunited for more picture taking. This time as a family.   Oh joy and jubilation! Triumph over tribulation! Elation from creation! Little Molly Margaret is born!

As I'm falling asleep this night, at home alone as I must be, I ask myself what one thing of all things I've learned on this day of trials and firsts. Curiously, it is that I finally understand woman's age-old hatred of war. After the gory ordeal is done, after expending all that blood and sweat, fluids and feces and prolonged suffering to bring a life into the world, why spend it so stupidly, so wantonly?

We live and we learn. Some days—special days like birth days—we learn more than others.

## May 14    *Crowing Day*

As I open the front door this morning to get the newspaper, I find a bulging plastic bag on the porch. Stuffed with? "Dy-Dee" reads the blue type on the bag's side. The ever-resourceful Timarie's work. Nine days ago she arranged for this particular diaper service after checking the vendors' prices and policies. On Monday, before I got home, she must have phoned Dy-Dee to activate service. What timing!

For me this is crowing day—that wonderful day between the baby being born and the baby being brought home from the hospital. Dad can brag about and take credit for his newborn without having to feed it, change it, or listen to it cry.

So, with my pink "It's a girl!" button pinned to my best blue suitcoat, I'm off to school to strut before faculty and babble my joy to my magazine production class. About a third—most of them young women—clearly share that joy, while the rest seem skeptical or puzzled. Clearly, my age is not that of the usual excited father. Many in my audience are doubtlessly interested not in having babies but in avoiding having them. No doubt, too, they have trouble reconciling this happy laughing professor with the crafter of nasty midterm examinations and ill-tempered critiques of their writing assignments.

In any case, I can hardly wait until the school day ends and I can get back to the hospital. On the freeway words erupt in rough, excited bursts:

What a happy day in May
When little Molly Margaret
Came to us to stay,
Not trailing clouds of glory
But love to show the way.
Little Molly Margaret,
How trippingly off the tongue
Come those words for this elfin girl
Whose time on earth has come.
I say her violet eyes
Are two of one of a kind,
And the smiles I give her now
She'll one day repay in kind.

Poem or the day's doggerel, that will have to be decided in some future reworking. Perhaps I'll have it polished by Molly's fifth birthday, then present it to her. With God's blessing and my nagging, she'll be able to read by then.

Timarie has Molly at her breast when I arrive. Mom's feeling tired and a little sore, but the little pink Molly is a balm for all that. Timarie may hold the baby virtually at will, and it takes practically no time at all to have her wheeled down from the nursery in her mobile crib. A new baby boom is said to be underway, but you wouldn't know it by our hospital. Only one other baby girl and a baby boy share the nursery with Molly, and the scarcity of new parents and visiting relatives and the small number of nurses on duty keep the halls clear and make for a more relaxed administration. Visiting hours and access-to-baby times are definitely more flexible.

Further evidence of the this local lull in baby production is that the three other beds in Timarie's room are empty. This makes it all the more

cozy and private for our steak-and-champagne candlelight dinner, an added inducement in the hospital's birth-with-us package. Happily, there's an alternate selection to the steak. (Second-generation fathers have to cut down on their red meat intake if they want to be around to see their daughters married.) It's chicken Kiev, and it's...well, not bad for hospital food. The champagne is even better. And the company—Timarie across from me, and at her side our daughter sleeping in her see-through plastic cribette—is best of all. New mothers give off a sublime glow, and it's worth a year of life to bathe in it when you can.

Timarie recounts the day's visit by her pre-selected pediatrician, Dr. Hsin Chang, who has pronounced Molly a healthy newborn. To complete the circle of satisfaction, Timarie pronounces Dr. Chang an excellent choice of pediatrician. Why not? Tim chose her from several she had interviewed, both on the phone and at their offices. Her criteria? Was the doctor board-certified in *pediatrics*? Did the doctor have privileges at multiple hospitals, including at least one emergency hospital? What hours was the doctor available? Were the hours flexible? Did Tim like the nurses in the doctor's office? How long had the nurses been there? Did the doctor give unsolicited advice during the interview? Did the doctor check every new baby, even when not on-call? What was his or her fee schedule? Did the doctor treat the mother-to-be as an intelligent person who could be spoken to openly, plainly? Above all, did the doctor believe in breastfeeding—something Timarie was deeply committed to?

Dr. Chang, whom I have not as yet met, passed with flying colors, and gave off "good vibes" to Tim, too. A very thorough and professional mother, my wife. Even before she had a baby.

Before visiting hours end I go to the nursery for a last day's look at my Molly, who sleeps innocently in her cribette, with a felt Minnie Mouse doll at her head, the hospital's way of identifying her as a girl child. (Boys get Donald Duck.)

She is so small, so delicate, so...feminine. I'm turning to jello when I realize a woman in her sixties is studying me from just off my right elbow. I turn warmly toward her. It's time for sharing.

"Is that your granddaughter?" she asks, smiling.

My day is over, done.

"No, that's my daughter." Too sharp for the occasion.

Anyway, my balloon implodes. I go home to sleep, alone with my years.

# May 15   *Molly's Homecoming*

At school I'm in my final hours of crowing on this last day of regular classes. Luckily, I have two today and get to gloat twice. Again, I look at student faces for reactions. Again, most of the young women seem interested, and I'm asked about name and birthweight and eye color (I've already volunteered that she's a redhead). The males, with the exception of an appreciative few who say such things as "all right!" and "way to go, old man!," are all business. Get on with the lecture. I do, impatiently, because this is getaway day...when the family spends its first full night together at home.

At 4:16 p.m. I'm at the hospital, helping Timarie pack and loading the car with more paraphernalia than a supply sergeant can steal. I've already belted the borrowed new Dy-no-Mite infant car-carrier seat in place, in conformance with that wise California law which requires such safety devices for the newborn from the first trip on.

At last all is stowed, and a nurse's aide wheels bottom-sore-yet-buoyant Timarie down the hall, Molly in her arms. I lead by 20 yards, ready to attend to that most frightening of all hospital experiences: "The Paying of the Bill." (What do they do if you're short, take the baby back?) To my very brief amazement, the total is a paltry $84, easily settled by Visa.

Timarie asks to see the tab. "All this fun and excitement for only $84!" she pipes up. "And we get to keep the kid, too?"

The cashier laughs politely, and a bit nervously, I think. She's probably heard via the grapevine about this particular patient's Monday night broadside.

Even as I'm signing the tab, though, I realize the rest—the remainder of hospital charges, the obstetrician's final bill, the anesthesiologist's, the lab work, etc.—can't be far behind. In truth, I've already done some preliminary figuring, and even with the best and most expensive health insurance available to me, Molly's delivery will run to direct, out-of-pocket costs slightly in excess of $1,000. I can't help but compare that to the two-for-one bargain price of about $250 I got in 1967. How do young Americans without good insurance afford to procreate these days? Ask not your president or Congress....

At home Tim puts tiny Molly on our king-size bed for a diaper changing.

"Ready to get some practice for the summer?"

"Why not?" sez I, wondering if it's really like riding a bicycle. Molly's bottom—unlike her vagina, which is disproportionately large, as I've been warned in the prenatal classes—is so small and even the smallest pre-ordered diapers from the diaper service are so large, that the change is clumsily made.

"A little rusty?"

"A lot rusty...but it'll come back."

"Remember to work the washcloth under the lips...and always front to back."

"So I hear."

I work the cloth slowly enough that it might be interpreted as hesitant.

"Does it bother you at all to clean her vagina?"

"No," I lie. "Not much," I add, backing off. In fact this first-of-a-lifetime experience has left me feeling strange, almost guilty, as though I've violated my infant daughter's privacy in some way. I believe even the freest and strongest of us remain, to some degree, prisoners of our generation. Mine was sexually naive and repressed, and none but the most-favored young males (and I was not among them) could expect to see a vagina-in-the-flesh before they were at least 17—if then. It was also a generation, like it or not, that fostered in the mind of boys the attitude that all females—except one's mother and sisters, who were sacred and somehow different from all other females—were targets of opportunity, to be hit on whenever you had the chance...no matter the consequences.

I've probably indirectly and unknowingly passed on this dubious wisdom to my sons. I'd like to think I civilized it a little, though. In handing out condoms with my frank sex lectures, I also let it be known the skins were for avoiding pregnancies as well as disease. With less conviction, I told them that sex was best when accompanied by caring—if it couldn't be love—for the partner, knowing such words at best are only theoretical to young males with the usual hormones rampaging through their bodies.

But now the tables are turned, as they say in the movies. I have a daughter's virtue to protect. "For yourself?" our now-irrelevant neo-Freudians might ask. And why not let them ask it? Otherwise we'd have to dump them into the already-overflowing unskilled labor pool.

OK then, who am I protecting Molly's virtue from? Probably some small male child out there somewhere on the planet, toddling and burping, who may one day father a child by my little Molly. When I tell Timarie what I've been thinking, doubting that it would have occurred to her, she says it need not be another baby, but maybe a young first-time father pacing around a nursery just as I did when Timarie was a toddler.

Possible. I had never thought of that. Such circularity. In some ways today's women are way ahead of yesterday's men.

So much for speculation about the future. This night Molly will sleep in our bed, between us, since her cradle won't arrive for a few days. Once Timarie's father brings it, we'll keep it at our bedside—for the first month at least. Possibly for the summer. That way we can keep close watch on our helpless charge.

That is the plan, but Molly has no use for plans right now. No use for much of anything—including the newly come-in milk that has swollen Timarie's breasts. We brush Molly's cheek to trigger the head-turning response, and put the nipple to her lips to initiate the sucking response. So much for the vaunted basic instincts! Molly cries with the tit in her mouth, when it's out of her mouth, when Timarie massages milk out onto her lips, when we tuck her down between us on the king-size bed.

Timarie is beside herself with worry about Molly starving. The authorities say that a normal newborn needs 55 calories per pound of body weight a day!

Why won't she nurse? Is it that sitting upright on a painfully hard, unforgiving mattress, her mother can't get the right angle? I can't figure it either. Has Molly forgotten how to suck? She didn't wail this way in the hospital!

Tension burns me out before 11:00 p.m., and I join the dead. Timarie's keeps her awake and sitting on her stitches, in great pain, weepy until the wee hours of what she will call her "longest night."

A typical first night at home with baby, we've heard.

# May 16  *Some Tardy Nesting*

Here yesterday, gone today. Molly and Timarie are off to her mother's house for two days because Molly was early and the carpets were late and the house, quite frankly, was a jackstrawed mess when we got home yesterday evening. This morning the rug men arrive and begin their prep work, while I paint the floor moldings ahead of them, then go on to do the walls and closet of what will be Molly's room. According to the experts, pregnant women are supposed to give in to a nesting urge along about their eighth month. In a flurry of energized activity, they make ready a comfortable place for the new arrival. Timarie insists that through some quirk of nature, or perhaps because I've overdosed on prenatal classes, *I'm* the one that's nesting.

Maybe so. Anyway, some major changes in the household were necessary. With four grown people and a dog living in a three-bedroom house, my 19-year-old son Karl, who works full time and goes to school part time, has had to move out and in with buddies, leaving his room for Molly. Kurt, his twin, who goes to school full time and works part time, will stay and help keep house. The dog, Prunella, who has been sleeping half the time in Karl's room and half the time in Kurt's, will stay in Kurt's.

I'm worried about Prunella. She's into her twelfth year and along with her growing physical infirmities, including a walnut-sized tumor in her neck, she's developing a shortness of temper with small children, as became evident six months back when Timarie's niece visited.

A more manageable concern are the fleas resident on Prunella (who can be dipped) or in the carpeting (which is being replaced); we'll have to have the house and yard sprayed to head off a major summer infestation, but that of course will have to await the laying of the new carpet.

At 9:42 p.m. Timarie calls from her mother's with good news and bad news: Molly is feeding regularly and well, now that Mom has improvised a procedure of priming Molly with water through a nippled bottle, then switching to the breast; Mom, however, is hurting down below. "An episiotomy is not all it's cracked up to be," she puns. Though her sisters have gone out and bought a Sitz bath and an inflatable plastic donut for her to sit on, and she's taking Tylenol with to-the-minute regularity, the fundamental pain remains.

## May 17  *Resolutions Made*

The carpet is going down and looking just as great as I claimed it would when Timarie and I shopped for it. She favored a darker charcoal gray which wouldn't show the dirt, but because it only came in the jute backing, she let me persuade her to go along with Irish Silver Frazee, which looks dazzling.

Molly's room also sparkles, now that the rock-and-roll posters are down and the wall's spackled holes are covered with the antique white semigloss, which glosses over the wallboard's many wounds.

Now to the trim. With an uneasy Prunella and the transistor radio—tuned first to the Angel game, then the Dodgers'—at my side for company, I paint away and think of tomorrow's reunion.

It's not as lonely as it might be, though, because I can count on Timarie calling every two hours to give me a progress report. Molly's fine, feeding regularly, sleeping well, and getting a lot of attention from Tim's five sisters and three brothers who have been dropping by to marvel over the new addition. Mother fares less well. Stitches itch when they don't hurt, and her first Sitz bath was "a pain in the butt."

After a dinner of toast and canned chicken noodle soup, I make a list of other necessary tasks to be completed this summer:

- Refinance the house.
- Buy one—maybe two—new cars. (Both Timarie's '69 Cougar and my '79 Omni have over 115,000 miles on them and are showing unmistakable signs of senility.)
- Shop for a new personal computer and printer.
- Paint the living room, dining room and hall.
- Fix the leaky shower stall.
- Put a new lawn in the backyard.
- Resurface the driveway.

And then, of course, the *hard* work.

- Mind the baby.
- Final polish a novel that's about ready for publication.
- Complete four poems that have been in limbo for nine months.
- Re-do my syllabus and course plan for Journalism as Literature.
- Keep a journal of my summer with Molly.

The seventh day approaches and I think I'll rest.

# May 18      *My Plan For The Journal*

**M**olly's back! So is Timarie, who has brought her parents, Margaret and Art. Art in turn has brought the much-used family cradle, all cleaned and polished for its new occupant. We place it in the master bedroom next to the California king-size bed, where Molly will be near us and carefully listened to over the coming nights.

Orlando, a good friend whom we've got our eye on for future godfather duty, also drops in to see the new addition; he brings Molly an elaborate mobile that plays "Over the Rainbow" as a yellow bird rides a swing against a multi-hued plastic rainbow. A future infant stimulator if there ever was one.

The house is still a clutter of out-of-place furniture and unstacked books, and I haven't even had time to prepare dinner. So we make it a short-but-sweet homecoming/natal celebration with a bottle of Dom Perignon—one of two bottles given to us before our marriage, the one we didn't take to Ireland.

I scramble some eggs and warm some homemade five-day-old chili for dinner as Molly, wrapped tightly in a receiving blanket and blinking at the flashes, is passed from arm to arm and Tim and Art take the obligatory snapshots. Then we break up, and I pour some milk for bed-bound Timarie.

With Molly in her cradle for the first night, sleeping beside me, I tell Tim my thoughts on the journal idea, and what I would put into it. Of course I would try to sell it...the mind set of one who spent five years as a full-time free-lance writer doesn't just evaporate. And certainly what I had to sell was no every-day story: Fifty-two-year-old former magazine editor and free-lance writer comes in from the cold to academia after his 20-year marriage falls apart, then remarries a 25-year-old former student, in Sligo, Ireland, with a pickup cast, where he's talked her into going to make with him a literary pilgrimage to pay respects to his favorite poet, William Butler Yeats, then on to London and Paris for the honeymoon, and nine months and one day after the nuptuals the little girl they worked and planned so long and hard to have entered this world, to be cared for the first six weeks by the both of them in concert, and the next two months of life primarily by her old man, who had three sons in his first generation but never a daughter. Yes. "I am content to live it all again"...as a second-generation father of a daughter.

Well, whatever the commercial possibilities, the journal would have value as a family record, something Molly could read long after I'm gone and maybe know me better than she would otherwise. It would be *our* book—belong to the three of us, a brief record of a special time in our lives.

Ground rules? Purpose?

First, I'll be completely honest. Anything important that happens—if it's germane to the story of Molly's first three months—will be included, though naturally I'll avoid repetitions in the interest of brevity.

If I blow the whole experiment—if the summer turns out to be a disaster—I'll say so.

If I have successes, I'll brag about them.

If the strain gets too much and I give in to uncharitable thoughts, I'll write down what they were.

If I feel supersentimental, I'll let the whole maudlin mess hang out.

I'll speak plainly and frankly on bodily functions we distance from ourselves with the words regurgitation, urination, defecation.

Furthermore, I will put down and pass along anything I learn—insights, tips, shortcuts, observations—that might be helpful to others caring for young babies, knowing from long experience how hard it is to do much that's right.

Additionally, I will try, within my powers, to make the journal entertaining reading. If it should seem pretentious, tendentious, mawkish and smart-alecky, remember that style is the man. I'm a pretentious, tendentious, mawkish, smart-alecky kind of guy, Molly me girl. And I'm too old to change.

Finally, I hereby agree that, if I should abandon the journal and decide not to go through with the above, I will nevertheless carry on as Molly's-minder and happy homemaker over the balance of the summer....Meaning I agree to clean the house, do the shopping, cook the meals, and do the basic busy baby work.

"Go for it!" applauds Tim.

## May 19 *Friends With Dinner*

Our friends Rod and Heidi arrive with dinner and their son Aaron, born April 15. Heidi is a former student of mine who lately has blossomed as a poet, something of a regular on the coffee-house circuit in Southern California. Rod, a high school teacher of both science and drama, has brought French bread, salad, a dry white wine, fruit for dessert and a succulent dish of cold salmon topped with his own special dill sauce. This is reciprocity for a cassoulet I prepared for them shortly after Aaron was born at Long Beach Memorial Hospital. Timarie and I certainly got the better of the exchange. Honesty forces me to concede that Rod is as good a cook as I. Probably better.

The talk, animated and peppered with multiple interruptions, goes naturally to recent labor and birthing experiences. I listen and suddenly realize the great difference in American parenting since I was a father the first time. Heidi and Rod and Timarie and I all participate in the talk, confess fears and tears and the joy that comes with being participants in the giving of new life. Not at all like the old days when Mom got wheeled into labor alone to wrestle with an uncooperative nature. And silly old macho, sheltered Dad got shunted to the waiting room, or the smoking room as it was sometimes known before the Surgeon General's report gained much credibility, where he paced and cursed and sweated out the fate of mother and child, whom he could not see until all the mysterious goings-on that were no business of his were concluded. Sometimes, if he were lucky and pleasant with the nurses, he might be shown the swaddled child through a glass window before it was consigned to the nursery for general viewing.

I can't help but believe family life is better served by this new openness and intimacy, that the ties between mother and father and child are stronger and less likely to unravel under the stress of housing and feeding and rearing in today's intricate urban hive. Surely it should have some lessening effect on the divorce rate as well; living together the pain and wonder of birth seems good training for future money squabbles and mid-life crises. Only time will tell, but fairly soon, I think, if the sociologists stay on their toes.

After dinner Timarie suggests we photograph the infants together. This necessitates moving Aaron from his Portacrib into Molly's cradle, a transfer that delights the parents but pleases the month-old boy not at all. Exclamations of "how cute" and such accompany the snapping of record shots, which show Aaron bawling alongside a serene, sleeping Molly.

Someone alludes to a failed first date as uxorious limits are met.

"She's small," Rod says, "but we may still have a match."

"She's prized as a great beauty," I lobby.

"And the dowry?"

"Two bullocks...and I'll throw in a goat."

Too much of that smarmy domesticity stuff and they revoke your racquetclub membership.

# May 20     *Cradle Watching*

A week old today, Molly conforms roughly to the normal newborn's eat-sleep cycle, nursing for about a half-hour every three to four hours, not missing that infamous 2:00 a.m. feeding, which seems more debilitating than I remember from the first round of fathering. The early morning drama keeps the three of us awake for a long hour—an unfair start to another round of changing, feeding, comforting. It's hard to believe Molly sleeps almost 16 hours a day.

Late this early afternoon I prove to myself that the old parental instincts remain, and that a father's care of a child can approach that of a mother's. This always-restless sleeper falls asleep on the bed with tiny Molly, the bare seven fragile pounds of her, lying limp on my chest. Two hours later I awake, without having budged. Neither has Molly.

I've read somewhere that this heart-to-heart contact may prevent Sudden Infant Death Syndrome. The thinking? That the parent's beating heart reminds the child its own must beat. I find the fear of SIDS lurks in the back of my mind. No matter that it's only a longshot possibility. I'd take any precaution to ward it off. I suppose my fear derives from ignorance.

Timarie is a lot more knowledgeable than I. She's been taking classes, reading, talking to other young mothers....But she confesses that she, too, has the same fears and must periodically peek in on Molly in her cradle to be sure she's breathing. Indeed, we catch each other sneaking into the master bedroom for reassuring checks about every other hour.

The decision to keep Molly in our room goes beyond our merely wanting her close to us, where, typical of over-anxious new parents, we can watch her. Her room, or what will be her room in three or four months (now it serves as our all-purpose storage room, holding an unassembled crib, unworn baby clothes, gifts of toys not yet played with, the carseat when not in use, diapers of various kinds in stacks and boxes, and a bumper crop of laundry baskets), faces west, seaward. Therefore, it is subject to greater ups and downs in temperature. To compound matters, it is also rather far from the thermostat that regulates our central heating, and in any case represents too long a nocturnal walk to read a wall thermometer, even if we had one.

Yes, Timarie and I have boned up on "neonatal cold syndrome" and the chilling dangers to our daughter. There are so many ways—conduction, convection, evaporation—a baby can lose heat, and once cold it is so hard for it to create and conserve it, that special care makes sense.

Experts recommend a room temperature of 68 to 70 degrees; the temperature under the baby's clothes, of course, should be warmer—over 80 degrees for at least the first two weeks. Swaddled, tightly wrapped babies, with plastic pants over their diapers, stay warm. But changing wet diapers or bathing the baby necessarily means exposure to the ambient air, and that can lead to trouble. Trembling and twitching tip one off that the infant is burning vital calories in an attempt to stay warm. Moreover, the baby has only limited fuel to burn, and must soon get its heat from outside. Once chilled, it must be warmed (by a parental body, perhaps?) before it is wrapped in dry clothes; otherwise the garments hold the cold *in*, and that can spell tragedy.

# May 21     *The Perils Of Nursing*

Tim's hurting top and bottom. More up top, now. Her nipples are dry and cracking. Molly is rough on them. Though she gets almost all her milk in the first dozen minutes of feeding, she doesn't stop there, sharing with most babies the need for extra sucking, which she does with a gusto made audible by her lip-smacking and her mother's squeals of pain.

Timarie tries to fob off a pacifier (prepared for everything, she bought two of the orthodontic variety a month or so back) on Molly. Won't work. Molly gums it for three seconds, then spits it out and howls.

"You can't fool that girl," Timarie says with begrudging admiration.

Maybe not. But the problems now begin to multiply.

Molly regurgitates the mid-morning feeding; a trace of pink stains it, obviously blood from the mother.

Timarie is upset. I'm concerned. While I do the diapering and baby back-patting and kitchen-cleaning, Tim takes to the phone, seeking counsel. A lactation nurse tells her Molly is taking too long to eat, which really sends the new mom into a tizzy; it means Molly is not getting enough milk. Margaret reassures her daughter that if a baby is wetting six to eight times a day, then she's getting enough to eat. A representative of the La Leche League tells Tim over the hotline to relax . . . she's too tense. That makes her tenser.

When Molly throws up another, pinker feeding just after noon, Timarie becomes alarmed. She fears the little girl will lose what precious little weight she has. A phone call to her friend Mary at work, who has a six-month-old daughter, provides reassurance through a handy illustrative exercise: Take a tablespoon of water and throw it on a counter; yes, the spill looks like more liquid than it is, just as the spat-up breastmilk seems to be more than it is.

Timarie finally connects with Dr. Chang, whose morning has been absorbed by a hospital emergency. Her advice: Air-dry the nipples for a half-hour after nursing; rub them with A & D ointment; drink at least three quarts of liquid a day; don't worry about the baby not getting enough to eat . . . if she isn't getting it, she'll let you know in a not-to-be-mistaken way. The continued, or increased, presence of blood in the breastmilk would necessitate some changes, but for now, try not to worry.

## May 22       *Keeping Track*

Off to give my final final exam. Home late in the afternoon to read the results. Timarie is feeling feverish, but it doesn't stop her from attending to her new responsibilities as a new mother. Attending isn't the right word. She flat out attacks them, with her customary thoroughness. After she and Molly have gone early to bed, before I can get dinner prepared, I find next to the chair she uses to nurse this up-to-date log of the day's major events:

| Molly Wakes | Molly Eats | Molly Sleeps |
|---|---|---|
| 2:20 a.m. | 2:23 a.m. | 3:18 a.m. |
| 6:50 a.m. | 6:52 a.m. | 8:15 a.m. |
| 12:40 p.m. | 12:50 p.m. | 2:20 p.m. |
| 4:49 p.m. | 4:53 p.m. | 5:35 p.m. |

Exhaustion is a general condition of the household, time a gift in short supply. We're all asleep by 7:50 p.m.—but lightly. The next "Molly Eats" isn't far off.

# May 23  *A Formula For Complications*

Timarie wakes up really sick. Her temperature is over 101 and she's experiencing sharp uterine pains. I bring her cold packs and we take turns comforting the baby and making phone calls, to her obstetrician, his nurse, Molly's pediatrician. We both worry that there's serious trouble inside; she may be hemorrhaging.

She gathers her strength. Then, when Molly falls asleep after her mid-morning feeding, Tim drives to Dr. Keel's, while I stay with the baby and fret for an hour and a half.

Timarie returns.
The good news is that she isn't bleeding to death in her innards—the pain comes from the uterus contracting back to its original size. The bad news is that she has a breast infection, visible in a wicked-looking web of red streaks across her left breast. It's staph, a bacteria that has entered the cracks in the nipple from the baby's mouth and thrives on mother's milk.

I'm off to the pharmacy for antibiotics.

A check with Dr. Chang brings instructions that Molly not be nursed as long as Timarie's temperature is over 100; otherwise the risk is great that the infection will be passed on to Molly. We should resort to formula temporarily. But what brand? Tim relays the fact that the larger part of my life I've lived with an allergy to cow's milk and its products. Then use Isomil (a soybean formula), the pediatrician advises.

I'm off to the market for formula.

Timarie, meanwhile, mans the breastpump to express the staph-infected milk. There are three reasons for doing so: get rid of the bad stuff; avoid the quite painful complications of breast engorgement; encourage the gradual increase in the production of milk—another example of the body's use-it or lose-it policy.

So far my wife has been spared the much-discussed postpartum blues. Rather, her general condition might be called postpartum elation. But not now. She's down.

While Molly wails in the bedroom, I blunder through the formula mixing—two ounces of sterilized water for each spoonful of Isomil. I first make an emergency bottle, then go into mass production, filling and capping enough three-ounce nursing bottles to last two days anyway.

When I bring in the bottle of formula and Molly takes right to it, Timarie's mood further darkens.

"What's wrong?"

"Depressed."

"Because you can't nurse her?"

"Because she's getting milk that isn't mine... and because she likes it."

"It's just to tide her over."

"I *hate* Isomil."

By 10:00 p.m. I'm beat, though I have much school work that begs doing. I ask Timarie how she's feeling.

"Better," she says.

"I have a vested interest in your getting better," I tell her, "not only because I want you to be well, but also because I can't get a thing done while I'm tending the babe."

She smiles. "Now you appreciate the time I've been putting in."

# May 24     *Ever Thankful For Small Favors*

Another drudge day! I've got half a ton of term papers to read and I can't find my reading glasses. With the aid of antibiotics and aspirin, Tim's improving, but I still must change Molly, feed her formula and burp her, put her down and pat her to sleep. It tears me apart to hear her cry, so I tiptoe around her cradle when she finally dozes off.

For the evening meal I broil spareribs, which are tasty enough, but son Kurt dumps his semi-chewed bones into a paper bag on the kitchen floor. The ever-clever meat-thief Prunella waits until eyes are turned and then stealthily drags them out for a final working over.

Drags them where? To the new carpet, right in the entryway, that's where. And the giant grease stains resist the best that Woolite Spray Foam can do. I am livid. One week to the day the Irish Silver Frazee was laid!

Late at night, as I'm just about to fall asleep, Timarie asks, "What was the best thing that happened to you today?"

"You got better," I say sleepily.

"That's nice. And finding your glasses had to be the second."

# May 25     *What's In A Name?*

Timarie feels much better, which is at least fortunate this day, as a veritable parade of friends drop by to "ooo" and "ahhh" over our little Molly Margaret, dropping off enough presents to fill a dresser, which they will. I should amend that they're all Timarie's friends. Is that because I have no friends? Possibly, though I prefer to think it's because her generation is interested in babies as mine is not—except, perhaps, as grandchildren that, thankfully, can be enjoyed in moderation and from a safe distance.

Among the females Tim's grown up with, she is the first in this sager age of family planning to experience motherhood. So they come, curious and solicitous and generous and genuinely loving, asking questions—most of them about what labor's like. I feel privileged to be with these women and the very few young men; I'm rather awed and puzzled by what seems their boundless capacities for charity.

As for my contemporaries. . . I have no illusions. Most of them think I've gambled away my forebrain at the racetrack, or lost it to drink; why else would a grown man of my advanced age choose to marry a 25-year-old woman (that's not so hard for some of the guys to accept) and go through fatherhood again?

I've explained to a few of them that I never had a daughter, that I love children, that I fear death, that I've always viscerally believed that a good God would never finance my purchase of the farm if I had a little baby to care for. (Only a couple of takers on that one.) Also, that I truly prefer the company of children and dogs to the adults I've generally associated with. Which is reason for them to say I might have some psychological problems—minor, and no doubt treatable.

My soundest argument, for which there's no rebuttal, is that having a child or not having a child is not my choice alone. What of Timarie? Is she to be denied motherhood because I feel I'm too old? Not fair, is it?

In any case, the totality of it all has brought me face to face with one bona fide self-revelation. I have gone through five-decades-plus of life thinking I was the norm by which others' eccentricities were measured. Only now have I faced the overwhelming evidence that I am the eccentric, not they. If so, I will make the most of it. One look at Molly's face tells me that *I'm* right.

This evening, with mother's milk from the day's final feeding trickling out of the side of her mouth, Molly looks up at me with beetled brows and incredulous eyes.

"Can't believe an old guy like me could be your Pap, can you, Molly me girl?"

"Don't talk that way," Timarie reproves.

I know that Molly is just learning to wonder as far as her rapidly maturing eyes will take her, and she is not stunned by the improbability of my being her father.

"Little Otto will *really* have a problem," I add to needle Timarie. I refer to our running joke on my choice of name for Molly's future brother. In fact, had by some mischance—some longshot upset of near-certain probability—our child been born an XY boy, I suggested Otto as a name during our first discussion of the subject. Why? My favorite Dutch Uncle was named Otto. It's also a good, strong masculine name. It has the magical property of being spelled the same way forward and backward. And it means "rich," which, if only for its talismanic value, should not be overlooked by anyone in my family.

Timarie gives me a controlled smile.

"There will be no Otto," she says, as she has said two-score times before. Why? I didn't say Ivan! What is so terrible about the name "Otto?" It's preferable to David or Lance or Ricky or whatever other cutesy *prenom's* in vogue! Isn't it?

# May 26     *Memorial Day Traffic*

On this day redesignated by our citizen merchants Memorial Day, Molly makes her debut in the world of affairs. We've been without a couch since Karl moved out; I told him to take the sofa if he could use the bulky monstrosity that always hurt my back but seemed to have another 30 years of wear in its salt-and-pepper fabric hide.

Timarie has set her mind on a leather replacement, and so we're off at midday to "The Leather Factory," which has a sale going. I'm not much of a shopper, unless we're after imported beers or domestic wines, but Timarie makes up for all my deficiencies. For two hours and 12 minutes she tests and tries and questions and subtly haggles over a sofa, and then a chair, that have caught our fancies. All the while we pass Molly back and forth as she naps in her Napsak, an ingenious child-carrier that straps over your shoulders and allows you to rest the infant on your chest or your back. I should add that we pass her back and forth gently so she won't awaken and with her hunger cries bring all the store's business to a halt. It doesn't happen. Even when the bargain is struck and we've committed ourselves to $1,860 dollars-worth of an antiqued-burgundy buttontuck chesterfield and cane-sided chair and start the drive home, we get no more than a brief string of irritated whimpers, then sleep.

After we're home and unloaded, Molly still slumbers in the car seat, which I set on our bed.

"Should I wake her to feed her?" Timarie asks.

"Let sleeping babies lie," I say, drawing on 20-year-old wisdom.

In case she missed that saw, I offer another. "You know what I always say about babies, Tim. If it ain't broke, then don't fix it."

# May 27 *A Spring Offensive*

Timarie's mad as hell and she's not going to take it anymore. This morning she found a flea on Molly's head. She also has two fleabites on her own ankles.

Fortunately, she won't have to take it anymore if the fumigators, who come today, live up to their promise. They'll spray the yard and house, and, if after 12 days fleas should remain, they'll come back and do it all again for free—until the pests are gone for good.

I hope they're right because it's such a hassle to cover all kitchen items and the babies clothes and accouterments—an hour's work anyway. And then we must vacate the house for at least three hours to avoid the insecticide. Timarie and I have decided to take no chances with the baby...Molly will spend ten to 12 hours with Timarie at her mother's place.

I, meanwhile, take Prunella to the vet to have her flea-dipped; she'll spend the night there.

Then I'm off to school to grade the last papers and turn in my final grades.

Kurt will open up the windows at noon to air the place out before he goes to work.

At ten this evening, Timarie returns with Molly, who is asleep but, according to Tim, has had a very cranky day. She seems alright now, though. It is I who comes down with a headache from the lingering vapors of bug-killer. Couldn't we come up with a better way of controlling insects?

# May 28     *Slipping Away For Commencement*

It's commencement day, and so I'm off to school to serve, as I usually do, as a faculty marshal. That way I get to see the final product of our educational process and say my last "goodlucks" to the graduates on the appointed day of ceremony. But in the sun-striped quad this late May mid-morning my mind drifts to Molly, my own little girl I hope to see graduate one day. As the begowned grads file up to the outdoor platform to receive their sheepskins, I keep trying to picture Molly in my mind....red hair, broad forehead, violet-blue eyes, tapering chin, bright old-ivory skin, long fragile limbs. I decide to skip the reception and hurry home to check my portrait for accuracy.

So many friends and relatives have pronounced her cute or beautiful that I've dropped my guard against the subjectivity I find so sickening in doting new parents. I've come over, been converted. Indeed, I have dubbed Molly "Miss Neonate of 1986." It has a nice music to it, and I've fallen in love with the word "neonate." How like the medical profession to abandon words like "baby" or "newborn" for such Latinate pomposity.

I must get one of those yellow diamond signs to hang in the Dodge. Not with the non-specific "Baby on Board," but with "Miss Neonate in Car."

I must also read more on the care of babies, now that my commitments to my students are met for another semester. Timarie and I have settled on three: *Dr. Spock's Baby and Child Care*; Penelope Leach's *Babyhood*, second edition; and Frank Caplan's *The First Twelve Months of Life*.

Each is comprehensive, comes highly recommended. Together they should give us answers to the questions we will be asking over the next several months. I pray that they are not questions born of an emergency.

# May 29      *The First Rite Of Passage*

**M**olly can be contrary and gets her way with a persistent forceful cry that sounds out, "a'naa, a'naa"—the accent on the second syllable. When quiet and awake she seems quizzical, wondering, absorbing all through her beetled brow.

At 2:17 p.m. Timarie calls me to the bedroom with a muted but excited cry. I enter to find her holding up some small purplish-brown something.

"Uh?"

"The umbilical cord!"

I realize, as Timarie reaches into my nightstand and drops the now-useless desiccated flesh into the empty felt box my wedding ring came in, that Molly has gone through her first rite of passage. It also means she can now be given a real bath, instead of just sponging her, tiny part by tiny part.

This evening, after taking in the *McNeil-Lehrer News Hour*, I enter the master bedroom and peer at my sleeping daughter. She's changing daily, I know that. Yet I don't see the changes until they accumulate into a "leap forward" perceived after the fact. I regret that. And I have no idea what's going on in her fresh mind, either. I regret that, too. But she's no unfeeling, unthinking blob; I know that!

# May 30  *A Day Of Several Firsts*

This busy, busy day begins with a bath. Molly's first. Timarie actually administers it, while I stand by, a worried backup, as the delicate operation is conducted in our bathroom sink, which is lined with a large yellow sponge that has an infant-shaped recession bigger than Molly scooped out of it. Despite the cushion, I fear that she's so tiny and slippery she'll not get through it without one dropping. I find myself holding my breath during the more ticklish maneuvers, which include cradling her chest in your hand while you wash her backside, tilting her head back for rinsing the rusty stubble fuzz of hair we're praying she'll keep, and the actual transferring of the cooling wet body from the sink to a waiting towel wrap. But it is all done without mishap, and probably in far shorter time than it seems to me.

On to Dr. Hsin Chang, Molly's doctor, whom I meet for the first time. She's a calm, studious middle-aged woman—just the one to answer our anxious questions. We're delighted to hear Molly's heart is sound and ticking along just perfectly. There is some slight concern about the weight, however; no doubt the interruption of nursing because of the breast infection has had an effect on her present seven pounds, eight ounces. Feed her on demand, Dr. Chang advises—and bring Molly in for a weekly weighing.

Any other questions?

Timarie has her list all ready:

How many bowel movements a day is natural? (About 12 for a breastfed baby Molly's age.)

What should the color and consistency of the stools be? (A rich yellow watery paste.)

What causes diaper rash? (Many things...urine on sensitive skin, various bacteria, yeast, diarrhea.)

How do you treat it? (Frequent changing, as much air as possible, protective and preventive ointments.)

How many hours of sleep should Molly be getting a day? (About 19, or thereabouts, is normal.)

Any questions from Dad?

Just one. I'm concerned because Molly's fontanelles seem overly small to me, and I don't want her brain constrained in any way.

Dr. Chang assures me Molly's soft crestal spot is in the normal size range.

"And you can take her on walks now," the doctor adds.

That's good to hear.

Next it's on to James Publishing, the law book publishing firm where Timarie works as Marketing Director, to show Molly off. The exhibit is a complete success as the infant is passed around, ready hand to ready hand, with Timarie perkily alive in the shower of compliments. Jim, her boss, who's wife is due in four months with their first child, gets a turn. So does her friend Mary, whose own pregnancy predated and overlapped Timarie's, and with whom Tim has shared maternity clothes and prenatal tips, not to mention, now six months later, the birth of daughters. Teresa, Tim's best friend, from college days, who peered in on Molly her first night in the hospital nursery, gets to hold Miss Neonate last and longest.

A busy day, but nice.

# May 31    *The Family That Walks Together*

Our first walk together...Molly and me, and Timarie makes three. Technically, it's not a walk, I guess. Molly's really being carried, in what is rapidly becoming our indispensable Napsak. Bobbing with her little head is a hand-knit yellow bonnet, a gift from Luise, a German friend; spring mornings are usually chilly in Southern California.

We settle on a mile-and-a-half hike through out neighborhood, Timarie toting first, then me for the home half. I am particularly pleased that it's a success, that the waif drops off into contented sleep almost as soon as she's zipped into her cocoon. Only when we halt to switch burros and lengthen the shoulder straps to fit does she fuss and cry. Carried, or riding in a vehicle, newborns love motion. Must go back to their days in the womb when mother's movement was a comforting constant. In any case, Molly and I are cleared for heavy use of the Napsak in the months ahead.

As I untruss her at home and the perspiration drips from my nose down on her cotton snap-around undershirt, I marvel again at her beauty. Most everyone says she looks like me, and that's what I still can't get over. Through the months of pregnancy I had hoped she would look like Timarie and not be burdened with my dolichocephalic head, my bumpy angular face, prognathous jaw, too-generous nose and the supra-orbital brow ridges that some distant Neanderthal ancestor cursed me with.

Well, she's got my mother's red hair, Timarie's Celtic skin, eyes that are a blend of the both of us.... As for the rest, what can I say, except that on her they look good.

# June 1  *Molly Malone*

To stay Molly's fussing, I sing to her. Usually, it's our song, which happens to be, appropriately, "Molly Malone." I find her fascination with my performance (the first time my singing voice has favorably impressed anyone, to be sure) beckoning me on into six or eight encores.

I should add that I now stay with the first verse exclusively. "In Dublin's fair city, where the girls are so pretty, I first set my eyes on sweet Molly Malone" seems to have been written for my little girl. The second, which begins "She was just a fishmonger, and sure t'was no wonder" seems a lot less suitable. I have nothing against fishmongers. They ply an honest trade. And I have nothing against cockles or mussels, alive or dead. But I do feel Molly is cut out for a loftier profession. Maybe a philosopher, or a concert pianist.

As for the last verse, its first line, "She died of a fever, and no one could save her," speaks for itself and is thereby eliminated from my repertoire. I don't need any of those downer thoughts.

# June 2 *O Happy Day! O Silent Night*

Miss Neonate has slept through the night, God love her! Slept six and one half hours straight, without need of that terrible two-o'clock feeding. We are hopeful. We also confess to waking at 2:03 a.m. and several times thereafter, worrying why she hadn't awakened, peeking into her cradle to see if she was still breathing.

One thing sure...she recognizes the tit in the morning. The sight of it brings lusty grunts and a warm-up working of her tiny oval mouth. She can somehow scoot up to six inches across the bed to get to it, even though her means of locomotion is limited to writhing on her back. Amazing, and humbling, this will to live. To grow.

To assure that, I find myself increasingly concerned with Prunella. Specifically, with the old dog's behavior. I can't do anything for Molly without setting off her jealous barking. Constantly, I find myself checking on Prunie's whereabouts, to be sure she isn't left alone in the same room as the baby. That chore, piled on top of burping, diaper-changing, Timarie-tending and house-cleaning sure doesn't leave me much time or energy for my summer journal. Not quite the way I had it planned.

# June 3  *Another Hitch On The Poop Watch*

That's what I've signed up for. Yesterday's rejoicing proved premature, as Molly awoke at 2:05 a.m. and let her needs be known. They had to do with bad gas and grass-green runny stools, an unsettling departure from the curdled golden product of a healthy breast-fed baby. As pediatricians tell you, the close study of bowel movements will give you a pretty good running line on your baby's health. We've already discovered that diarrhea and constipation are not mutually exclusive, and Tim has found that a lubricated rectal thermometer used to take Molly's temperature also, when gently twirled, facilitates the passing of gas and feces. Yet another way of helping her is to gently bring her legs up against her abdomen.

At 9:40 this morning an old friend of 19 years, a very macho hombre, calls in the midst of a diaper change to offer belated congratulations on the birth of my first daughter. He is father to one, a redhead also, grown now and studying languages in Europe, the deserved apple of her father's eye. My friend is somewhat surprised to find me home, and even more so to learn what he had interrupted.

"You don't mind being up to your wrists in shit again?" he asks with amiable brusqueness.

"Why should I mind when I've spent 15 years in corporate America with it up to my chin?" I think it's my best impromptu parry in a year, but my friend, with an office on Wilshire Boulevard serving the needs of other movers and shakers on the Fabulous Boulevard, chuckles weakly in essential non-agreement.

I know other parents find this fecal duty distasteful, and diaper-changing one of the more onerous chores of child-rearing. Personally, I don't mind either. Moreover, for one who had three babies within 15 months in the first round of fathering, and who remembers the time as being an arm-weary prisoner in the world's largest diaperpail, changing Molly is easy as pea soup. Like riding a bicycle, the art comes back with very little practice, and by mutual agreement, I'm getting a great lot of practice, because toward the end of this month, when Timarie's maternity leave ends, Molly and I will be alone together. And there lies another blessing in disguise... in the act of changing and diaper-pinning, Molly and I will only have eyes for each other.

## June 4  *Like Father, Like Daughter*

Molly's intestinal distress continues and it's becoming clear that something is amiss. Timarie and I suspect it's dietary—that what Mom is eating is being transmitted to the infant in the mother's milk. We've also got a good lead on what the offenders might be. Milk and egg allergies have plagued me most of my life, and the susceptibility to such substance intolerance is usually passed along within families. Maybe Molly—poor thing!—is the recipient of this lousy legacy.

When Timarie phones Dr. Chang and tells her of the problem and my history, the pediatrician advises Timarie to eliminate her own intake of milk and—curse of curses that I've suffered through so long—that means cheese and ice-cream as well. Timarie makes her decision. She will no longer drink nonfat milk, use it on her Nutri-Grain cereal, eat Haagen-Dazs, grilled cheese sandwiches or pizzas, etc. Talk about commitment!

This early evening I drive to the drug store for more Isomil, the soy-based formula, and Pedialyte, a solution babies under two are given orally to replenish body water and minerals lost through diarrhea. Some extra baby bottles—six- and ten-ouncers—are also in order. More nipples, too. And another breastpump, manual variety. (Tim doesn't like the batter-powered one she bought; it isn't functioning properly.) I fall asleep between 8:30 and 9 p.m., weighed down by fatigue and the gravity of approaching responsibilities, when I mind Molly alone by day.

There must be more to life than tired bones and laundry without end.

# June 5     *Matters Close To The Heart*

**M**olly and her stools are better already. But Timarie is worse. Though she has faithfully and scrupulously washed her breasts and hands both before and after feedings and blew them dry with a hair-dryer, the dread breast infection returns in full force, so hospitable is the environment of mother's milk and a baby's mouth to the offending organisms.

I mind Molly while Tim's gone to her OB. She's near tears when she returns. What's wrong?

Doctor Keel has said that with another flare-up she may just have to give up breast-feeding altogether.

"How long did you plan on nursing her?" I ask, as neutrally as I can. I attended a prenatal breast-feeding class (one of two men in a group of almost thirty) with her and know how intense her feelings on the subject are.

"I plan to nurse her for a year." Said defiantly.

"But what if you can't. . . .You know, it's difficult to do it that long. Even for a mother that's not returning to work."

'I am going to nurse her anyway." Unmovable.

"It's a great idea, but don't set your sights unrealistically high."

"Doctors are not gods!," Timarie snaps. "C students can become doctors."

I pause to let emotions settle. "Why do you want to do it?" I ask from a plane of detached curiosity.

"Why do fish swim?"

"Meaning?"

"Because it's so natural—so right!" she states passionately. "It's very basic to me. . .primitive. Besides, it's for Molly's health."

"That's true," I agree, remembering the first advantage our breast-feeding class teacher cited. The mother's milk-borne antibodies keep infants healthier for the better part of a year. Breast-fed babies also experience less diarrhea and less constipation.

"It's the closeness, the eye-contact," Timarie adds, softening, tears overflowing her eyes. "It's one of the most rewarding things I've ever done."

Who's to argue?

Back to the rut of Isomil and breastpumping unusable milk.

# June 6     *Play And Perceptions*

Timarie feels better this morning, and nurses Molly from the left, unaffected breast, while I prepare formula for the second morning feeding. No sooner are mother and child unlatched than Timarie picks up the breastpump to express milk from the engorged right one. I watch her pour four ounces of results down the sink. Yes, indeed, it's pure waste.

On this most appropriate day I teach Molly the game of "Ripcord," which I've just invented. Its mother in this case is Molly's fussing and crying. I hold her at rigid arms' length over my head, then let her have maybe 12 or 18 inches of freefall before the imaginary ripcord is pulled and I swing her in side-to-side jerks as she slowly descends on Normandy, played brilliantly by the living room floor.

Timarie thinks the game may be a little rough for Moll, particularly where her arms join her torso. Molly doesn't complain though. She opens her violet-blue eyes to their full roundness as her parachute guides her safely back to earth—and she stops whining! She stops whining! Reason enough to introduce her early to playing games.

I foresee pros and cons to this second-generation fathering. While I really do look forward to my excuse to renew acquaintances with Ernie and Bert, I doubt I'll ever be up to another game of "Candyland."

Dinner time, and I'm preparing stuffed peppers as I heat up some formula.

"Ummm! Something smells good," says Timarie, shuffling into the kitchen.

"Bellpeppers," I say.

"No, it's potatoes," she counters.

"Sorry, babe. Can't be. I'm not fixing potatoes."

Almost simultaneously we solve the mystery. The Isomil, so despised by Timarie two weeks ago, smells good, like potatoes. "Like French fried potatoes," Timarie admits sheepishly.

I volunteer to put Molly down after our dinner and hers. It's a formidable challenge to glide the tightly wrapped (odd how they like being bound) infant down the hall and gently lay her in her cradle with a minimum of hitches and unnecessary movement. Keep her calm, content, satisfied, before her eyes close.

The way to do that? Amazingly, the way they did it in the hospital. Putting in the infant's line of sight a rudimentary, black-and-white-on-8½-by-11 bond drawing of a faintly smiling, faintly female face. We were allowed to take this treasure home with us, and it continues to work its magic just six inches away from Molly's wide-open, concentrating eyes.

I say amazing because I didn't quite believe the nurse who discussed infant perception in our infant stimulation class when she said that a newborn likes black and white images best—especially if they happen to resemble the human face.

True enough. And I've got additional proof of the fact. Somehow, the mail-marketing people at Johnson and Johnson's Child Development Products Division got my name off some prospective parent list and pitched me in the eighth month of Tim's pregnancy to join their toy-of-the-month club. That's what I call it; the formal name is the "Play and Learning Guide."

In any case, answering to some latent spendthrift's yearning, I decided to splurge on my number-one girl and signed up, initiating a monthly shipment of toys that run anywhere from $10 to $20. First to come was Visual Display, two gate-folding plastic strips that interlock into a reversible cube, or break down into two free-standing triangles. Each of the 12 panels has a "picture" in black-and-white or color—a butterfly, target rings, smiling sun face, cat, dog, fish, unbreakable mirror, etc. I've spent hours reversing and shifting the various sides around, studying her reactions to the different images. Her hands-down favorite? A crude black-and-white face of a girl, very much like the crib companion she had in the hospital. Interestingly, her second favorite is a panel that reproduces nine of the twelve panels in miniature; the little girl's face is there, too.

I suspect there is another reason why Molly will stare at this particular side, with its Visual Display digest, long after she's become bored with the dog or the cat or the sun. Infants want variety, too, I've read, and here variety meets complexity, detail. Yes, little Molly is learning. So is her father...that one should never underestimate a baby's smarts.

What they know most likely exceeds what even the most daring pediatrician suspects. Such is the direction of knowledge since I was a college student. From a hundred billion galaxies down to classifying quarks by kind, everything now is older, longer, deeper, bigger, smaller, more complicated than we thought just a couple of decades ago.

Cruel that it should take us so long to learn how ignorant we are.

## June 7     *To Molly's Doctor*

This is Molly's first true day of marathon fuss. Nothing done for her—changings, strokings, feedings, rockings—seems to halt the crying. Why? Was it her walk (via the Napsak on Timarie's back) that tired her? I doubt it. Her cry sounds hoarse to me, but is that because of a chill (picked up on the walk?), or because she's cried so much? Her bowels are also loose, suggesting a possible intestinal bug. She has fed about every two hours—3,5,7,9—to the point of surfeit.

Timarie says she's in a growth spurt. I've heard of such things before from mothers, but in neither *Doctor Spock* nor *The First Twelve Months of Life* can I find any discussion of it. I do hope it is a growth spurt, if there is such a thing.

Doctor Chang, a steady woman, calms our concerns with a don't-panic, lets-just-observe-over-the-next-few-days approach, though she does express a minor concern of her own: Molly has only gained three ounces more than her birth weight, and this is her 25th day of life.

Anyway, the strain has taken its toll, and by mid-afternoon I've been chewed out for bad breath, non-existent dog hair on clothes, and using Tim's side of the sink in lieu of my diaper-filled one. So I scrub out a plastic pail for dirty diaper deposits, then give my son Karl—who has dropped by to do his laundry—the silent chill treatment for jamming the washing machine by overloading it. Most of all, I hope for better days.

# June 8  *Books For Molly's Future*

I awake today to see my wife and daughter in restored and, for a change, simultaneous good health. I also see evidence of the emotional nature of nursing. I kiss Timarie while she lies and feeds Molly, and the other nipple gushes milk. Amazing! Molly seems to sense an intrusion into her bond with her mother and gums her nipple the painful wrong way.

At midmorning we take our Sunday walk toward the ocean and find ourselves right in the middle of a neighborhood garage sale. Timarie can't resist garage sales, and neither can I when I find books are for sale.

As Molly-in-her-pouch earns the "aws!" and "oooos!" of the vendors, we acquire a copy each of *Charlotte's Web* and *Stuart Little*, four Judy Blume books, Ramona Cleary's *Ramona Quimby, Age 8* and *Ramona the Pest*, a hardback edition of *The Red Badge of Courage* and another of Edgar Allen Poe's *Tales of Mystery*—all for $2.25!

These will go to build Molly's library, already begun with a half-dozen Dr. Seuss books, a copy of *Mother Goose*, and Timarie's own cherished editions of Beatrix Potter and two children's literature anthologies.

I envy Molly the awaiting pleasure of discovering reading—the pure and private joy of it. And what if she doesn't want to read, you're thinking? Then I'll take an ax to the goggle-box.

## June 9     *Cries And More Cries*

What do you do with a crying baby,
>   What do you do with a crying baby,
>   What do you do with a crying baby
>   Early in the morning.

Timarie and I grapple with that great riddle of child-rearing daily.
"What did you do when you had three of them?" Timarie asks this a.m.
"I don't remember."
"How could you not remember?"
"I don't know. I just don't."
"Well, did more than one of them ever cry at the same time?"
"Yeah....I seem to remember that. One sets off another."
"Then what did you do?"
"Pat 'em, I guess. I don't know. My mind's a blank." (My mind—like most minds, I suppose—is merciful in not remembering pain. All I can say for sure is that the experience left me with an unnatural reverence for silence. It's not just worth its weight in gold. Toss some platinum and diamonds on the scale while you're at it.)

To find out what to do with our crying girl we consult the literature. It advises us to find out the "why" of the crying first. Hunger—and these steady, insistent cries become identifiable soon enough—is the most common cause. No problem: Feed the child. Pain cries are not easily mistaken either—sharp, cutting, urgent. Relieve the pain—often centered in the stomach or intestines, where a gas bubble wants out. Frightened or "overstimulation" cries, perhaps triggered by sudden bright lights, loud noises, violent movements, tend to be shrill, penetrating, and interrupted by long, trembling gasps for air. Fatigue or boredom are the causes of cries less easily read.

Whatever the root cause, most cries (the baby's sole means of communicating, after all) can be silenced with cuddling and rocking. (Penelope Leach recommends rocking through an arc of about three inches at the rate of 60 rocks a minute, or faster.) Babies just need to cling, and they prefer to be pressed to skin or soft, textured material.

Sounds good. But how long do you wait before picking up the baby for comforting after you've just concluded a crying episode? That depends on the parent's state of mind, which in turn depends on the time of day, time of the month, reserve of patience (if any), amount of recent sleep, the direction of the stock market, whatever. And while the hunger, boredom, fright and pain cries can be responded to with ameliorating measures, tired or bored cries seem to defy silencing. I find that I can go a maximum of 14 minutes of crying before I must pick her up; Timarie can barely stand five.

I concede my wife's the better as well the more putty-hearted parent. Wisdom and mercy both decree that if picking up and cuddling a baby will stop its crying, then by all means do so. Timarie's philosophy is that Molly will know plenty of sadness, frustration and the truth that each of us is alone, after all. No need she learn it this soon.

God bless the good folks at Graco for making their "Swyngomatic," and bless Tim's friend Mary for lending us her sister-in-law's. This wonderful portable contraption is continuously driven by two C batteries and is adjustable in swing speed from turtle to rabbit. A soft liner with safety belt covers the seat, while up front there's a little tray with a scalloped red and a blue functionless wheel for turning, as well as room for other small objects to study. My stroke of genius has been to take her Visual Display panels and position them on the tray, so she has something to look at as she swings.

Molly likes her swing almost as much as I do. More often than not, head fallen to her shoulder, she goes to asleep at the vigorous rabbit pace, and I let her swing while I write in my journal. Timarie doesn't quite approve. But what can I do? If I stop the swinging, the tike's head tilts over at a terrible angle, doing no good to the tiny neckbone, which is, of course, connected to her chest-resting headbone. Do I try to wiggle her out of the swing seat's narrow confines and tote her off to bed?

That's a lot like waking a patient up to give her a sleeping pill. So I tuck her blankets around, make sure her booties are on, and slow the swinging to the turtle pace.

## June 10   *Blunders Of A Bull Shad*

Timarie has gone gaga over her baby—dotes on her every waking moment of the day, and in her sleep I do not doubt. She hovers over Molly, kissing and cooing and powdering and pampering the little doll. She's an evolving advertisement for motherhood, a state she seems to have been born for.

Today she thanks me for "talking me into trying for her" on our honeymoon. It was in London, and she wanted to wait a few months before attempting to have children... have a little breathing space as it were. But I persisted.

Why not get going right away, I argued. Chances were that at my age it might not be all that easy for me to father a child—particularly at first or second asking. Sperm counts drop with age, and it might take months or years to connect. Besides all that, if we should beat the odds, the child would be born in May and I would have a summer to care for her.

Tim gave in.

In fact, I had done a little truth-dodging with Timarie in London. Fuzzed the facts a bit. While it is true that males normally face lower sperm counts with age, I had withheld evidence that I had a lot to lose before my fertility would be seriously compromised.

During my roaring twenties, while in the fifth year of a five-year tour of duty with the U.S. Air Force, in Salonika, Greece, I had consulted a doctor about my fertility. Through no virtue of my own, I had escaped paternity; was I sterile? The Greek doctor who scoped my sperm sample reported that "the little fellows are most abundant, and strong enough to swim the Atlantic." I was pleased, feeling both lucky and weighed down with a new and major responsibility.

More concrete, after-the-fact evidence of my potency would be that in the only six months of married life that I've been freed of membranes and potions meant to prevent the propagation of my kind, I sired four children. One might correctly surmise by now that I'm proud of it. And those that offends can go to hell on a Mexican bus line!

Yes, I'm testy on the point. I suppose that stems from a frustrating social evening a couple of months back. Timarie, in the eighth month of her pregnancy, and I were at a typical Southern California party where few of those in attendance had seen each other before and most likely would not do so again.

After two gins and an hour of chitchat, I approached my wife, who was in lively conversation with a learned USC professor of studied modesty and his gracious and intelligent and very-with-the-movement wife. They were discussing a PBS television documentary that Bill Moyers had done and they all had seen (I hadn't), in which the journalist interviewed absentee fathers and welfare mothers; a handful of us listened as one black dude got roundly castigated by Professor Savant's wife. Seems he had bragged to Moyers about fathering a number of children he didn't have the intent or the means to support. "Men were just naturally supposed to give women babies" was a patchwork paraphrase of what the contemptible chap had said.

My third gin bade me appear for the defense. "While it is true the man's conduct was wrong," I said, "one can nevertheless appreciate the direction he was coming from."

"Oh, could one?" It was Mrs. Savant, a self-confessed mother of a boy and a girl (the proper number and division), with her blade out.

Yes, I said. Many men—some might call them natural men—took great pride in their fertility, which might in fact be the poor and untalented man's creativity. It was, after all, a life-giving, creative impulse being expressed. (I could talk professorese, too).

Professor Savant's wife gave me a smile worth one Nancy Reagan might flash upon being introduced to Daniel Ortega. "Excuse me, I should be mixing," said the lady as she made a quick exit.

Then Professor Savant, in his practiced Aristotelian manner, quashed my idea with a quick, short platitude and stepped off after his wife, leaving me in an embarrassing wake of silence. The auditors vanished like sea foam. And I was left in that most uncomfortable of all (including great physical pain) human states—not being understood, and with no opportunity to explain the validity of my argument.

Right, that's why I've spent so much space getting it out here. I want approval....Or at least understanding. Three more cheers for D.H. Lawrence and Knute Hamsun and Andres Segovia! Yes, and I'm proud to be as potent as a bull shad!

## June 11    *Ferris Wheel*

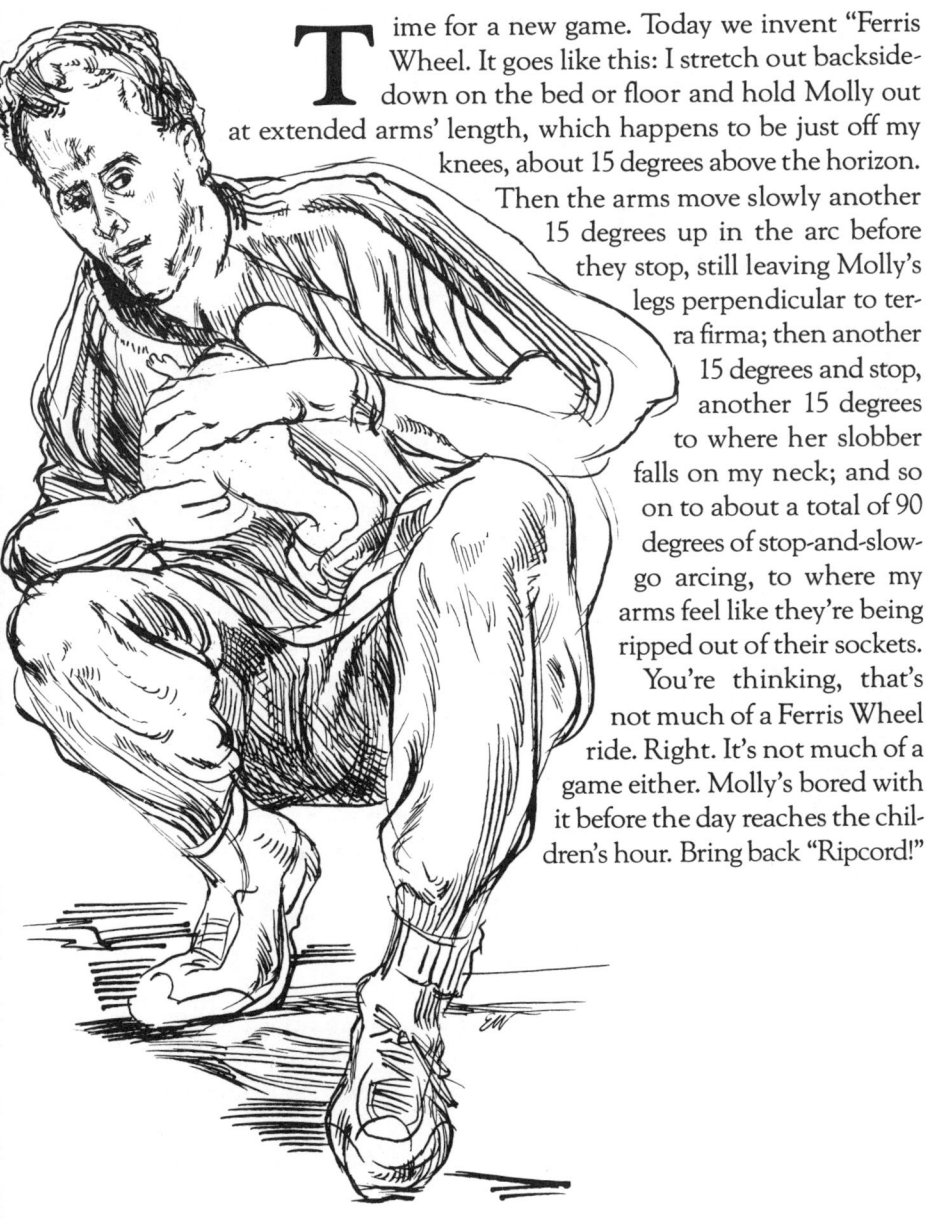

Time for a new game. Today we invent "Ferris Wheel. It goes like this: I stretch out backside-down on the bed or floor and hold Molly out at extended arms' length, which happens to be just off my knees, about 15 degrees above the horizon. Then the arms move slowly another 15 degrees up in the arc before they stop, still leaving Molly's legs perpendicular to terra firma; then another 15 degrees and stop, another 15 degrees to where her slobber falls on my neck; and so on to about a total of 90 degrees of stop-and-slow-go arcing, to where my arms feel like they're being ripped out of their sockets.

You're thinking, that's not much of a Ferris Wheel ride. Right. It's not much of a game either. Molly's bored with it before the day reaches the children's hour. Bring back "Ripcord!"

# June 12     *In Neptune's Hold*

This evening Molly goes to her first bar. Well, maybe that's stretching the term some. When you first see Neptune's Locker, a suds-and-sandwich emporium about the size of a boxcar and wonderfully placed on the western base of Huntington Beach's celebrated (largely by surfers) pier, it may look like just another beer bar by the sea. No big deal. Yet folks crowd it every evening, shine or rain (when it's actually at its best) to watch the sun set.

Neptune's Locker is popular with lovers and loners of all ages, ocean-worshipers too old to ride its waves, poets alone with their feelings, grizzled and taciturn veterans of life's roller-coaster—all students of sunsets who seek out this cozy, glass-enclosed watching spot at 1/100th the cost of doing the same in a Malibu bistro.

In the past I've spent some fine, solitary, reflective evenings perched on one of the Locker's 21 polished pier-piling-sectioned stools, looking out beyond the rose-foamed breakers at the sun's drop into the western sea. And I probably would have spent more if it weren't for the cigarette smoke and the fact that the bar beer is Coors, a brew which, to my well-educated palate, ranks on the taste ladder a rung below Budweiser and a rung above yak urine. Couldn't they try Moosehead?

The Coors is just fine by Art and Margaret. Timarie's parents are Neptune's pleased guests for the first time tonight. With a little wait, we've all managed to find stools at the L-shaped bar for the late-spring sun's red Pacific plunge. Molly's misses it, tucked away in the Napsak napping—except when Timarie can't resist yet another patron's request to show her off, and her little rusty-fuzzed dome and blinking eyes are exposed to neon light and cigarette smoke.

Timarie decides to give her folks a walking tour of the pier while I hold Molly. A great idea...for ten minutes. Then Molly decides Neptune's Locker is not her kind of place. She lets loose with a scream that could cut glass—and will drive the regulars out into the chilling dusk if I don't do the right thing.

It takes me ten minutes of squalling-infant taming, aided by Art who wraps his jacket around Molly, before we find the women. Art thinks she was just cold. I think she was making a statement. She'll probably grow up and revitalize the WCTU.

## June 13   *Fear Of Dying*

Friday the 13th. Molly is one month old today, and as I look into her morning-bright face I'm convinced she recognizes me. At least for the moment, in some erasable way.

The anniversary hasn't hyped me as I thought it would. Rather, it's spilled some morbid old baggage I've carried around for as long as I can remember. What if I died? This day? Or a year from this day? Or a year after that? Would Molly remember anything of me? Anything about me...what I was, how I felt, how much I loved her?

Probably not, science says. But on this head I won't accept science as the last word, because I don't think the method has yet come close to the last word. Somewhere in her there must be imprints of me—thoughts she'll have and delight in and know whence they came, emotions she'll know derive from somewhere back in time but are linked to hers, sorrows similar to those felt before her, flaws and failings she got in the genes, and joys and virtues that are not hers alone but a remnant of the man who gave her life, merely experienced in a later time and an altered setting.

I suppose the same can be said for my mother and father, and Timarie's mother and father, however unlikely that may seem to either of us.

The sorrow in this summer is that the moments of love and laughter are bittersweet for the father because they will be unremembered by the daughter.

Timarie returns in the late afternoon from a shopping expedition, snatching Molly from me as I sit in a living room reclining chair. She bubbles, enthuses, effuses motherly love for her child.

Prunella, who's been watching all from her chosen station by the patio door, starts her familiar medley of envious whine-barking and comes rushing toward my now-empty hands. While watching Tim bounce Molly in the air, I reach down to stroke the old gal. I cringe. The walnut feels like a tennis ball. I run my hand farther back from her neck to find a leash of smaller tumors beneath her black coat; they're spreading. She must be terminal.

A cat strays into the visible backyard dusk and in an adrenalin-fueled instant Prunella bolts out through the doggy door in hot pursuit. Am I wrong?

# June 14     *Death Watch*

I am not wrong and I have my answer. When I get up this morning and start outside for the paper, Prunella doesn't emerge from Kurt's room, her bedchamber for the last few months. I peer in and see an inert, bloated facsimile of her. Incredibly, the tumor in her throat has gone from tennis-ball size to grapefruit-size overnight. Death is near, and all the mind games and like evasions are banished by the sight of the dog in her grotesque proportions, robbed of any dignity. I place her on an old cotton blanket in the middle of the living room, stroking her coat as I begin the death watch.

Molly, for the first time since she's come to me, slips to the rear of concerns. I call the vet and describe the symptoms. All along I've prepared myself for driving her to the desert and, alone with my .22, doing her the quick justice of not having to die alone among strangers from the state or county government. But that's not necessary, the vet informs me. I can be with her at the end, right at an animal hospital a mere two miles from my home, and the violence of bullets is completely unnecessary. The lethal shot of barbiturates is mercifully quick and painless.

I jot down the address. But I drag my feet about taking her. Instead I phone both Eric and Karl to tell them their dog is dying, and that if they want to her see her a last time they should hurry. Eric can't make the long drive from the San Fernando Valley; Karl's close by and comes to pay his last respects.

In the late afternoon, as I take photographs of her for the record, something I can one day show to Molly, Prunella seems better, able to get to her feet and slowly move around. Maybe I was right about waiting.

# June 15     *Fathers' Day*

Hope deceived me again. When I rise at 8:05 and head for the driveway to fetch the hefty Sunday *Times*, I hear the faltering patter over the entry-way tile, then the porch concrete, of Prunella's feet behind me. I look back to see her trailing drops of blood from an immense open wound on her neck. Astonishingly, the tumor has exploded in bloody show, leaving a huge, dark-red-ringed hole in her neck. Behind her, in Kurt's room, as I will discover later in the day, she has left a two-foot-in-diameter pool of blood on the carpet, where she went to sleep when he got in at midnight.

My hoarse cries for "help" bring my son outside, where we do what must be done. We carry Prunella to the front lawn and wrap her in a blanket. I go back inside and call the animal hospital and tell them we're coming and why, then Kurt and I lift the alert but confused animal onto the back seat of the car. Only once does she so much as whimper, and that is when my trembling hand slips and strikes her gaping wound full on.

It's seven minutes to the animal hospital. We gently lower Prunella to the waiting room floor while my Visa card is first checked for being hot or abused, then pressed into the sliding device and a tally of $85 is ballpoint-penned in. She now has the the financial establishment's clearance to die with dignity.

At 8:41 a.m. she does just that, while Kurt massages her hindquarters and I stroke the unbloodied part of her newly deformed head and neck. It takes only six seconds after she's injected in the paw before her brown eyes, fixed on me, seeming to ask for an explanation, glaze over and her neck and head suddenly go slack and roll 90 degrees to the right.

She's gone. Kurt and I caress the heavy lumpy mass of white and black fur and worn-through-to-the-skin spots for another minute or two, too choked to speak.

"At least we were there at the end," Kurt says on the way home.

"And she got to travel more than most dogs do," I add.

Kurt reminisces about our houseboating trips to Lake Powell, Lake Mead and Lake Mohave, where Prunella had the chance to go semi-wild in a natural world.

Yes. She had 11-and-a-half pretty good years in our fold, and three boys to love and, for a time, look after.

Those who speak of dogs' deaths as though they were human deaths turn off some. Doing so somehow seems a major failure in humanism. And yet, while it seems to me the grief should be at least qualitatively different, who's to prescribe what another feels, or where our mammalian class sympathies should end?

If I were truly objective, which I don't much care to be, I'd probably admit that Prunella wasn't much of a dog as dogs go...not in the eyes of others, anyway. We got her out of the pound when she was four weeks old for Eric on his eighth birthday, picked out from an expendable litter of six Labrador-and-Dalmatian mixed bound for imminent extermination, not because she was the most alert or the prettiest pup there, but because when she saw Eric she approached him from inside her cage with a wagging tail, as though *she* had done the choosing. Instinct directed her to her boy, and the vet's caveat that she was born with an abdominal hernia, where the grape-sized lump of innards that popped through the outer sheath of muscle would probably one day be a problem, was a risk we swept aside.

She developed terrible skin allergies and became a needy, high-strung animal, hyperactive and neurotic...that is to say, she became a member of the family. She also remained a runt version of her at least bifurcated ancestry, an advertisement for neither breed. She always looked more than a bit ridiculous with her close-to-the-earth body, rotund in the Labrador way, with too-large ears and rather stupid eyes. I made matters worse when, in my meddling, domineering way, I canceled out Eric's appropriate name for her, "Collar," after the white circle of fur that nearly ringed her neck, with my own "Prunella Pimperton," after a ludicrous late 1940s' comic strip character within a comic strip, Fearless Fosdick's wizened old spinster love, which stuck and made her a laughing stock among both those who understood the allusion and those who didn't.

Prunella was an accomplished sneak-thief, a stealthy pilferer of meat left on unattended plates or in garbage cans with unsecured lids. She brutally uprooted any treasured plant we set out—begonias, azaleas, bleeding hearts—for reasons we never quite fathomed, while leaving weeds and geraniums completely untouched. A weird Labrador who actually hated water, she stank of her skin problems an hour after a bath and became an accommodating tenement house and public transportation to generations of otherwise homeless fleas.

Then there was the plus side. Her gentle nature, so good with my roughhousing young boys—with everyone in fact, including one visiting burglar. And she was tough when it came to colliding with cars. She was run down by two of them, and the second accident left her with metal pins in a leg and a hip. Her loyalty knew no limits, and went nicely with her strong sense of duty, which called for chasing all intruding birds and cats off the property with a great show of resolve. Finally, her capacity for giving pure, no-strings-attached love, most of it transferred from her boys, when they grew up and found other interests, to me, and she became jokingly known in the family—until Molly—as "Dad's only daughter."

I suppose you could say I became her "default love," as she became mine for a brief hard time in my life. Loneliness makes for unlikely matches, between men or women and pets, as it does between men and women who go through enough rejections and rebuffs to give up finding their Prince Charming or Snow White. And these default loves become a boon, if not a crutch, for both parties.

With all these maunderings out, I should also simply add that the dog loved me, so I had no choice but to love the dog, with all her faults.

I tell myself that death is a natural rounding out of life, both natural and necessary. It rounds out what must be closed out in the lives of amoebas and those of stars. But the depression won't go away, even after Tim cooks me Chinese chicken in red sauce and gives me a Father's Day manicure and pedicure, the first renewal of regular service since Molly's arrival.

Why does the gloom hang so heavy on me? Could it be that Prunella's last look was telling me that I am next, which in fact I am, the oldest living member of my extended family. Is it because I know I have less stomach for it than she, fear that I will face it with less courage at the end?

At an early evening diapering Molly looks up at me and, for the first time, smiles, broadly, clearly, unmistakably, at me, for me. On Fathers' Day.

## June 16 *The Smell Of Parenthood*

Kurt plays the Navaho early this morning. Before I even make it to the garage he's given away Prunella's 40-pound bag of Chuckwagon, and even buried her hoary droppings in the backyard—a chore I've been nagging him about for weeks.

But I still see signs of Prunella wherever I look: the exhausted leather leash hanging in the closet with license and chain collar, the orphaned fleas making panicky jumps from the carpet, the grease stain from her face on the doggy door, left there from countless emergency nose-first chases after marauding cats.

Mourning has at least two antidotes. Work and the transferring of affections to someone new. I spend the morning and half the afternoon in close touch with Molly—feeding, changing, stroking, cooing, cavorting—until I'm almost late to an appointment with the young designer who's working on my logo for Calafia Press. I make the meeting dressed in pleatless blue cords, huaraches, and a powder blue tee-shirt emblazoned on the chest with the gold block letters "UCLA," my alma mater, and stained on the upper-right burping shoulder with the crustal remains of "spit-up;" I smell more than faintly of mother's milk gone sour. Not quite what the up-and-coming publishing executive wears.

The sensitive young man sizes things up. Or else he knows that the customer is always right. "I guess burping comes first," he says. It does. Early and often. But I've never understood why. And though I'm going through my fourth tour of backslapping-duty, I still have a hard time believing that burping is really necessary.

## June 17     *Attack Of The Baby Acne*

It has come as we've read it would. The ghastly attack of the baby acne—or whatever this skin disorder is properly called. Scads of rough red bumps and some with little white blistery heads have appeared overnight on our beautiful daughter's alabaster face and head—disfigurement enough to make us want to turn away visitors at the door rather than lock Molly in a closet.

Timarie has declared a unilateral moratorium on photographs for as long as the condition exists. "I don't *want* to take pictures," she says. Nor does she have any desire to take Molly out into the world—not since going to Lucky's supermarket this morning and being forced to exhibit Molly to friends of her sister Patsy, who works as a cashier there. Too embarrassing, she claims, even though she's been told by every mother she knows that the condition is both inevitable and temporary. Has something to do with the skin starting to produce its natural oils and the pores not yet in functioning order, apparently.

My job—in addition to the usual chores of a New Age househusband father—is to go to the pharmacy and pick up the medication Dr. Chang has prescribed following Timarie's concerned call that "it was just hanging on too long"—Nystatin Neomycin Gramicidin Triamcinolone, by name.

# June 18 *Posturings*

Mom nurses her still disfigured daughter this morning as I am driven to the computer keyboard.

I've been holding back on this observation for weeks now, both because I feel uncomfortable saying things that might be slanderous of my infant daughter, and because I wanted to study her more before I drew any conclusions. Now I simply speak my mind because it is, at least to me, a revelation.

I believe that babies...well, let's say my daughter at least (I shouldn't allow myself to generalize from so few recent samples) acts, postures, plays roles to express her needs or get what she wants. There, it's out.

Her first and favorite role is that of Mademoiselle Tremblechin (pronounced "trambla-sha"). When she feels wronged or deprived, or is just sympathy-shopping, she not only wails but sets her little pointed chin into a rapid trembling motion that makes her look so pitiful your heart wants to crack. If that doesn't work to get more milk or caressing, she often shifts roles to Camille, the terminal consumptive with the shallow, heart-rending cough, which seems to have nothing to do with colds or the chill factor, but is alarming and very effective in melting down your resolve not to spoil her.

Empirical evidence tells me this can't be learned behavior, but a role given us to play at birth—or as soon as we are conscious of being social animals with needs we can't fulfill ourselves. Strengthening my case is a third role she has played—naturally and unknowingly, I believe—since she was old enough to see humans and objects external to her. It's that of Jungfrau Beetlebrow, the forehead-furrowed thinker-examiner, Aristotle's spiritual daughter, when she focuses on something new in her expanding world.

What do you think? What do the thinkers think? Am I dead wrong on this?

# June 19   *A Clean Breast Of It*

Timarie is depressed. Once again the breast infection strikes, threatening to end her plans to nurse Molly for a full year. I'm sympathetic, and I know better than to suggest she give up the idea. The commitment is rooted too deeply in her emotions for me to do anything but support her as I can.

By early evening, with the help of minimum-period ingestions of antibiotics and Tylenol, her temperature drops below 100 degrees and she's cleared to resume breast-feeding Molly.

She takes her favorite station to do it...a comfortable leather swivel-chair in the living room that allows her to cradle Molly in one arm as she nurses, and speak on the phone and sip a bottle of beer with her free hand. I like to sit on the couch across from her and watch the warm interaction between my madonna and child.

This seems a good time to raise a touchy subject: The feeding of Molly once Tim's maternity leave ends, which is less than two weeks away.

"What's the plan?"

"Keep doing what I'm doing."

Timarie's plan, already a week underway, is to pump what extra breastmilk she can (usually two-to-four ounces) whenever she can (during Molly's naps, when she's asleep at night), put it in disposable bottle bags, date it with a Sharpie marker, and freeze it for future use, for July preferably, when she returns to work, and not use it as we did this morning—as emergency rations during breast infections.

"Remember, I'll be pumping and freezing at work, too."

Yes, that's the plan.

But, what with Molly eating more each passing week, the probability is high we won't be able to sustain her long on breastmilk alone. Our fallback position is to mix Isomil with the stored breastmilk for the daytime feedings, then return her to the tit early mornings and in the evenings.

"You're still determined to nurse her a year?"

"Absolutely."

# June 20 *Aaron's Christening*

Our contribution to the potluck dinner for Aaron's christening is fruit salad, and it rides in the back seat with me and Molly as we drive to Rod and Heidi's duplex in Long Beach. Their invitation said the rite was to be "informal;" others might call it "unconventional" or "secular," still others—from another generation—might use the word "bohemian," because we've all been invited to read something, a poem or something else appropriate, or otherwise perform. Timarie, who drives, is a radiant mother about to make another debut with her daughter, whose baby acne is mercifully on the wane. Mom's dressed in a gauzy white summer dress decorated with lavender-colored roses, and she's dressed Molly in what she calls her "little yellow newborn dress."

In the warm peach dusk of the backyard, we sit in a circle, 11 strong. The poet Gerald Locklin is here and charts the course by reciting one of his own poems written for Aaron, followed by other guests who read favorite passages of prose, or slip in a quote from scripture. When my turn comes I must apologize for having nothing original for the occasion; I've been dry and haven't finished a poem in a year. So I read Hopkins' "Pied Beauty" and "God's Grandeur," old favorites that when I read them make me feel like the Jesuit the nuns of my childhood had hoped I'd become. Rod closes the formal half of the informal evening by playing his guitar and singing "Forever Young" and "Lullabye for Amanda" to Aaron. Rod has a fine voice that honors the words.

A hard-core seven of us retreat inside once it's dark. While Heidi and Timarie nurse Aaron and Molly, then put them down together in Aaron's cradle, the rest of us, with glasses seldom empty, talk of babies and travel and poetry and politics—but mostly babies—until midnight. Without doubt, the most convivial and enjoyable christening I've ever been to.

# June 21     *First Day Of Summer*

**W**hat an ungrateful little imp to choose this morning to add a new edge and more amplitude to her crying! Doesn't Molly realize I put in a long, hard night celebrating the arrival of her generation?

Why does my head feel like the gameball from a Mongolian polo match? Because I drank too much a) beer, b) wine, c) cognac, or d) all of the above. The correct answer is d.

So let's make this Dad's day off. I'll get me a major-league-baseball-game-of-the-week fix and then to bed. That's how bacchants celebrate the first official day of summer.

# June 22      *Competition In The Home*

I'm taking Molly out for daily walks in the Napsak now. She prefers to stay burrowed in the bag with nothing but the very crown of her red head exposed to the light and air, dozing to the soothing but rough up-and-down of my gait. Occasionally I'll unzip the bag to exhibit her to curious pedestrians, and I'm learning to ignore such remarks as that from an elderly woman today that "it's nice to see a man take his grandson on walks."

Maybe her vision was faulty. Molly's features seem to me to be as feminine as they come. Granted, she's lost some of her birthday hair...but new has come in, and in the same red color, as we had earnestly hoped. Maybe the thin or bald patches lead viewers to think they're seeing a boy child. Whatever, I certainly don't look a day over 45...well, maybe 50. Obviously, I time our walks for when Molly's freshly fed. A mile from home is no place to be when hunger hits. Even at home, when it's chow time, no amount of my roughhouse bouncing or nonsense-mouthing stays her hunger wails. Time for Timarie to take over this fine Sunday.

Timarie asks me if I'm jealous about her most-favored-person status. Do I object that Molly prefers her to me? I tell her I have no say in the matter. Love is love and finds its way.

I am quietly busy with a biannual cleaning out of the master bedroom's closet, regretting its shrinking size and the steady increase of garments I never wear yet can't throw out, while Molly, pink face up, sleeps on the big bed, and next to her Timarie, barebreasted, rests, rapt because she's listening to "A Prairie Home Companion."

Know your rival, they say. For me, that's easy as drawing breath. American Public Radio sends Garrison Keillor into our usually happy household twice every weekend—a Sunday matinee encore just in case a stray word got past us on Saturday night.

It's all in the open. Timarie has several times confessed her Platonic indiscretions to me. But this time it goes too far. Garrison is singing a "hymn" he wrote to the largo movement of Dvorak's *Ninth Symphony*, and as I turn away from the closet I see milk flow from her breasts in time with the melody.

"Well *thank you!*"

Her eyes are brimming with tears. "It's so beautiful," she sobs through trembling lips.

"Yeah, you get to hear his words," I say, fortifying myself with the high probability that it's the dead Dvorak's music and not Garrison's lyrics that have plucked her heartstrings so. "You don't have to do his laundry."

Thank God Keillor lives in Minnesota! Barring Murmansk, Californians will go anywhere before they'll go to Minnesota. I think I'm safe.

## June 23     *The Diaper-Rash Derby*

Sure, it's the foe of every caring parent, the now-you-see-it, now-you-don't, but-you-never-seem-to-beat-it diaper rash. Is Molly's so-fair skin especially susceptible? Or have I just forgotten what it was like during my first round of parenting?

In either case, Timarie and I are deep into the "Diaper Rash Derby," trying to find the ointment or powder that can go the distance. A problem is distinguishing between a rash that is caused by a yeast imbalance and the more common burn. Each responds differently to the different medications. Dr. Chang prescribed Lotrisone cream for the yeast variety; it seems to control the rash, but can only be used three times a day.

Johnson's cornstarch powder and Ammens medicated powder are both in the running for the burn, with the latter doing slightly better. Polysporin ointment gets its chance, at the suggestion of an on-call pediatrician. I've been championing Desitin, which worked wonders on my boys in the previous generation, but on Molly it seems to lack its old kick. Plain Vaseline petroleum jelly is a later, promising entry in the field.

Part of our problem, we've been told, could be the type of diaper used. Trouble is, we've also heard conflicting accounts on the virtues of cloth versus the newer plastic kind. We've been using cotton from the diaper service most of the time, though Timarie, fearing that Dy-Dee might be using too-strong a detergent for Molly's skin, has experimented with rewashing them in Dreft. No difference. We resort to Pampers or Luv's (6-to-14-pound size) when we're traveling or when we've exhausted our weekly supply of cotton.

At present, we have few conclusions to draw. It seems that the traditional cotton cloth is compromised by the plastic pants you put over the baby to keep the surroundings dry, while the newer plastic ones remove the urine from the skin but don't "breathe" as well as the cotton diaper alone. A temporary remedy we've employed when the rash is rawest is to put Molly in her crib on an oilcloth pad, with her bare bottom exposed to the air, hoping oxygen will works its wonders.

I'm sure Molly, who about every three days has some angry red welts on her thighs and bum, wishes the race were over.

# June 24  *Moonwalk*

Goodbye "Ripcord." Farewell "Ferris Wheel." Hello "Moonwalk!" Why didn't I think of this one before! Yes, it's played like it sounds. I hold Molly under her arms and and guide her through high and graceful slow-motioned leaps and bounds on the lumpy white chenille spread on our messy bed, which looks something like the lunar surface but admittedly smells more earthy. (It's where we change our daughter.)

Molly loves the game. And why shouldn't she? Haven't we all envied those astronauts who gamboled and cavorted with such delight on our television sets, their images transmitted to our living rooms across 263,000 miles of space? To be free of the harsh tyranny of earth's gravity! Wouldn't we all be happier and better people by just being weightless?

After the *McNeil-Lehrer News Hour* this evening, I bring Molly down to where I'm stretched out on the living room rug and let her try to wiggle her way over my chest. She delights in the play, suddenly spreading her lips and gums in a smile that just melts my heart.

"Come quick, Tim!"

She arrives too late from the kitchen.

"You missed the smile of smiles...10 on the Chernobyl Scale."

"Chernobyl?"

"Yeah, a complete core meltdown."

Timarie stares at me, penetratingly. "Don't you think that is rather tasteless?"

"Why?"

"Chernobyl was a tragedy. A lot of people were killed there."

True, and Molly's smile is the furthest thing from a tragedy. But hey! A meltdown is a meltdown! Sorry. Tasteless or not, Chernobyl is a keeper.

# June 25 *Exhibition Day*

I've made my special fresh fruit salad again for another family venture into local polite society. This 7-p.m.-soiree is one of the periodic reunions of Graceful Expectations, a prenatal and postnatal aerobic exercise program where gravid ladies keep their muscles taut for B-day, then return to tone-up and also show off their babies to each other and their spouses. Program directors keep track of class progress (human progress, in a small way, on a gym wall with Polaroid shots of before (the tumescent Mom) in the "Who's Due" column, and after (Mom and child) in the 'Who's New" department. Felt-penned in on a chart are the vital statistics of names, genders, delivery dates and birthweights, with C-sections noted.

I urge all prospective mothers and fathers to enroll in such programs; some health plans even cover part of the cost. First, it puts new parents-to-be in the company of others farther along in the family-making process. (I must admit I felt rather awkward at my first meeting—and not just because I was the oldest man or woman there by almost 20 years. It was just that I couldn't adjust to hearing grown men talking about amniocentesis and Kegels instead of the Rams or Dodgers. But I got used to it, got right into it. Babies are the one subject that brought us all together, after all.)

Second, and more important, are the health benefits to mother and child. Timarie credits her twice-a-week workouts deep into her eighth month of pregnancy with giving her the energy to carry Molly through to term—and the overall fine health of mother and daughter afterwards. A result just as important to Timarie is that her weight now, only one month after giving birth, is only two pounds more than what it was on her honeymoon.

Now that my bouquets are thrown, let me confess that I am not perfectly comfortable attending this reunion. In March Timarie conned me into going with her to "Coaches' Night." I reluctantly gave in and found myself one of only two men on the padded mat with 20 bulging females, and the only one nagged into actually going through the aerobic exercises. Stationing myself at the very back of the group did me little good because some frantic maneuvers called for turning 180 degrees, in effect putting the first last, and making the last a spectacle for all eyes.

There may have been other laughs, but I only heard Timarie's howl of hilarity drowning out the oom-tee-oomp beat of the music. I slunk off the mat and out of sight, swearing an oath to absent myself from all subsequent "Coaches' Nights." I might alibi that I had never done aerobic exercises before. The truth also must include that I am six feet four inches tall, weigh 215 pounds, have gout in the knees and arthritis in the neck and elbows, and even if you took away 30 years from my present age you would not find a flamenco dancer. Not even a fox-trotter.

This eve I take a seat on the fringe of the gathering, hoping I am not recognized as the Dancing Nerd by the mothers-since-March. I watch quietly as Timarie and the other excited mothers pass their children around, listen to their exclamations over how cute or pretty or alert each other's kids are. Young mothers are indeed generous with their compliments, but I have no reason to believe them insincere. It is in their natures to see beauty and promise in every child.

When Molly starts fussing and crying, Timarie gives her over to me, so she can take her turn eating the potluck offerings. (This switching has become a regular routine of ours at mealtimes). I am provided an excellent opportunity to leave my cramped station in a folding chair and walk Molly around the walls of the gym, out of the limelight. I do study the other babies, though, in my peripheral passes; five boys and six girls were numbers that nature could live with. And Molly, I conclude, is the prettiest and cutest of the lot...except perhaps for a ten-week-old girl who has the complexion of a Spanish queen and the biggest, roundest, most luminous gray eyes I have ever seen.

# June 26    *Where It Hurts*

My poor little Molly! Today Dr. Chang gives her a diphtheria-pertussis-tetanus combo shot and Molly screams in pure pain. Timarie believes the hurt was less than it would have been because, on her sister Maggie's advice, she gave Molly some Panadol just *before* the injection was given. It also gives us a jump on controlling the fever that accompanies the shot. Makes good sense to me.

Doctor Chang says to expect some swelling and overnight discomfort, and that's what comes to pass, alright. Tim and I have to be so careful of her left thigh in changing her; the slightest brush or touch brings back abbreviated versions of the afternoon's heart-rending cry. One useful precaution—Tim's idea—is to freeze wrung-out washcloths for about three minutes, then apply them to the leg while Molly's nursing or we're changing her. It does seem to help reduce swelling.

The dubious good news is that Molly sleeps deeply through the night, and that her weight, evidently stabilized, is up to nine pounds, four ounces. Only well after the fact do we learn that it's best not to let a baby sleep for more than four hours at a stretch after getting this somewhat controversial shot.

# June 27 *Play Ball!*

Daring? Yes. Ill-advised? Perhaps. Memorable? How could it be otherwise?

I have four tickets to the Angel-Indian night game, and Tim and I and Rod, Heidi and little Aaron and Molly herself are going to Anaheim Stadium. Play ball! If the babies fuss, the ladies tell us, they'll nurse them under baby blankets we're taking to the Big A.

It'll be Molly's first live sporting event. Sure, she's barely six weeks old, and her eyes can't even focus on the field, but maybe by just being there she'll absorb through the pores of her soul some of the abstract beauty and perfection of this finest game that man—surely with divine help—ever devised.

Eating, feeding, diapering, dressing, car-packing and driving take a little longer than we've reckoned. Much stadium cheering reaches us out in the parking lot. When we get inside and to our boxes up from the third-base line, we are told that the Indians have scored three runs on Mel Hall's homerun in the top of the first inning. Now it's the Angels' turn to bat.

The Angels show nothing. Neither do the Indians as all bats go temporarily silent. Molly, however, is not silent. In her Napsak, on my chest, she begins fussing and whining in the top of the second inning. And my drinking my first beer does nothing to quiet her in the top of the third. Her complaints reach an attentive audience within a radius of some four seats; there are a few frowns. I tell her that Aaron has been behaving like a perfect little gentleman, and that I prefer not to believe in innate human differences determined by sex. She's not listening.

What is much worse is that Timarie is growing quite ill. I feel her forehead and it's blazing hot. Is the damned dreaded breast infection coming back? She insists on our staying, but by the top of the fifth inning, with Molly thrashing and wailing in my arms, I decide it's time to go.

Molly didn't last as long as Cleveland's starting pitcher, who takes his lumps in the sixth when the Angels tie the game, while we're on the freeway. Back home, my ear to the radio, I listen as the Indians rally for three to win it. An exciting game. Nine runs scored, in all, and not one of them do I witness. Oh, well. Wait till next year!

Molly will learn to love baseball. We'll go to games together in my nonage. It'll keep her out of the goddamn shopping malls.

# June 28    *Eric Does Not Pass Go*

I was sharply and repeatedly warned against being a second-generation father. Wasn't once enough? Or am I some kind of pain freak?

At 6:06 a.m. this morning Eric, my 20-year-old son, wakes me with a panic phone call. He's in jail. He had three outstanding traffic warrants and had neglected to complete his motorcycle registration, so an unsympathetic judge has thrown him into Los Angeles County Jail. One side of me agrees with the judge that the boy needs to be taught a lesson in accepting responsibility, the other side fears for his safety because, from what I've heard, County Jail holds some hard cases.

Eric is desperate and wants me to pay his fines and get him out right away. Where am I going to get $660 when the banks are closed? He's already thought of that. It involves several people using their automated teller cards. I tell him I will have to think it over...my mobility is cramped...Timarie is ill with a fourth onslaught of the breast infection...the baby needs formula feedings.

His incoming calls continue, alternately cajoling and frightened. My suggestion that he stay in jail and thereby "work off" the fines sends him into another spurt of panic. If he doesn't show up for work he'll lose his job; that makes sense. He also says that assurances I've been given by correction personnel that he's not in the same cell as dangerous felons is bullshit—unless armed-robbery and coke-dealing have been suddenly decriminalized; my concern mounts. I tell him I will do my best, but I can promise nothing for certain.

Timarie sleeps most of the day. Molly feeds without complaint on a blend of Isomil and thawed breastmilk. I start my search for dollars.

# June 29     *The Bail-Out*

At half-past eight my son Karl and I set out for the big city for the bail-out. Our first stop is Hollywood to pick up half the bail money from Eric's mother, then it's on to downtown and the Los Angeles County Jail. The only time I ever spent inside such facilities was as a young reporter researching stories, and after just ten minutes at County I realize my life has not been diminished by what I've missed. Half the staff is bureaucratically civil, the other half is rude beyond belief. The problem, however, is that no two of them—civil or rude—give you the same answer to a question. Can we see Eric? Yes. Then no. Can we get a message to him? Yes. Then no. How much, exactly, is the fine to get him out? That, too, is subject to change, but the sum is finally set at $540, and paid. How long will it take for Eric to be processed out? About two hours.

At 1:10 p.m. I call Timarie and tell her what's transpired, then ask her how she's feeling. The wrong order.

She says she's feeling better physically, but she's clearly not happy. When will I be home? I don't know.

Karl and I walk to Olvera Street for a good Mexican lunch and a better talk, at the end of which we agree on the indisputable wisdom of attending to traffic tickets as they're earned—or avoiding them entirely—and, failing that, appearing promptly in court when one is summoned to do so.

Back at the jail we're told it will be another four hours before Eric's let out. (In fact, the number will eventually go to ten and a half, but I can't wait even the four, with Timarie ailing and minding Molly alone.) Arrangements are made for Eric's girlfriend to pick him up and we head south for home.

Timarie is out of sorts when I return in the late afternoon, no tonic for my already grim mood. She's feeling neglected.

I refer to the parable of Christ leaving the 99 to go after the one lost sheep to justify my long absence.

"I understand that, but it doesn't make it any easier."

"I only do my best." The defense has made its final statement.

The domestic air is chilly, and it has nothing to do with the night air. I'm feeling much put upon, from all sides and top and bottom, too; I'm also having serious—and tardy—second thoughts about the whole idea of having two families. Isn't one more than anybody can handle?

What I don't appreciate is that Timarie had special plans for this last day of her maternity leave, spoiled as it is by her ailing and my absence, and that she is deeply troubled at the prospect of being separated from her baby for the first time. Starting tomorrow.

Starting tomorrow I will be on my own with Molly during the day. Am I up to it? Ready?

If I thought so before, I sure have grave doubts now.

# June 30     *Not Just Another Working Mother*

Tears gush from Timarie's eyes. Her voice breaks into sobs. "I can't leave my baby. I can't leave my baby girl." Mom's all dressed and prepped for work but seems rooted to the bedroom carpet.

I try to console her. We've known all along this day would come. To give Molly what we want her to have we both must work. Besides, she'll only be away from her for six hours each day this first week back. And we're really luckier than most modern parents because I—not some strange babysitter—will be looking after her in the summers—particularly this first summer. The last argument seems the least persuasive.

Timarie leaves reluctantly, breast pump in hand, giving me specific directions on feeding and changing and washing. I swallow my pique at being told things I believe I've got down pretty pat and instead smile and say "yes, of course," and "I will, promise."

Molly and I are at last alone, one-on-one with an aggregate of only 11 ounces of frozen breast milk in the fridge; the rest of the painstakingly built-up store was quickly depleted during the weekend breast infection.

Timarie calls frequently to hear how things are going. Swimmingly, I tell her. I give her precise times and amounts because I, too, have had the wisdom to keep a log.

"Took walk from 10:10 to 10:40"
"Fed 3 1/2 oz. from 10:53 to 11:10"
"Fed 2 oz. 11:40 to noon"
"Fussy at 12:13"
"Asleep at 12:31"
"Awake 2:20"
"Fed 4½ oz. 2:26 to 2:38"
"Into crib at 4:09."
"Asleep at 4:14"

"Where's my baby girl?" asks an ebullient mom upon her afternoon return. She takes Molly in her arms and hugs her. She's glad to be back at work, but the greater joy comes with the reunion.

And I am happy to have completed my first day solo without mishaps or complications.

# July 1  *Ollalaberries*

**M**olly and I pick ollalaberries today in her first July sun. In truth, I'm doing the picking and she's doing the watching from her infant seat. She is content, as she often is, and I am serene, as I seldom am, warming and cooling to the dappling shifts of sun through the avocado tree above us. Even the stabs of the thorns are almost pleasurable as I try to glean enough of the drying purpling crop to make one more cobbler. Will the berry stains come off my hands?

My Molly purrs and coos and closes her eyes when the dancing sun patches catch them, fussing and smiling in infant-sudden ways, leading me to wonder if the alternating stimuli of light and shade is causing it.

My reverie ends when a black cat comes skulking through our Mexican orange tree. No lover of cats, I know this intrusion would never be if Prunella were alive. Thought leads to thought, and I remember her death and that last resigned look she gave me. Had Prunella been born to show me how to die? Would I, should I, do the same for Molly?

## July 2     *Tits And Trap*

A hungry Molly awakes on our California king-size bed at 3:10 p.m. and lets her needs be known. I lie down beside her and press her to me to comfort her. She roots around my bare chest, through the hairs, until she finds a dry shrunken dug. The betrayal is clear in an instant and she loudly bawls her anger and frustration. I tell her there are simply some things daddies aren't equipped to do. But she's not listening.

After dinner I tell Timarie of the experience and she deftly uses it as a cue for entering one of her classic games of "Trap." After complimenting me on how good a minder of Molly I am, she asks, "If you had breasts, do you think you'd be a better mom than I am?"

How do you answer that? You don't. You change the subject, as I did by chiding her for keeping her IRA in a bank's certificate of deposit account that's earning a measly six percent. "Roll it over into mutual funds," I tell her. "It would bring enough to send your son to Harvard."

"What about *my daughter!*" she snaps, sensing a sexist slip.

I'm too agile for her. "She's already graduated."

"From where?"

"The Sorbonne."

"In what subject?"

"In literature, of course."

# July 3     *Her First Dinner Out*

I have a faculty search committee meeting at school, so Molly will spend the day in Long Beach with Timarie's sister Patsy. It's to be my daughter's first time being babysat, and a nervous Timarie has seen to it that we are all properly equipped. I load into the car the disassembled Swyngomatic, the Napsak, the Igloo filled with frozen mother's milk, the diaper bag stuffed with all manner of items that just might be needed, the car seat with Molly in it—knowing that the process will have to be repeated for the trip home. It brings back less-than-pleasant memories of my first round of parenting, when the hassle of loading and unloading three babies and their impedimenta into the '67 Dodge Coronet station wagon seemed to take more time than the actual driving to and from combined. Welcome back to the grind, Pap!

When I pick Molly up in the late afternoon, I am rewarded for my trouble with a sudden smile—unmistakably of recognition—when she first sees me. And she's been a good girl on her first day away from her parents, according to the report.

This intelligence emboldens Timarie, who joins us at 6:00 p.m., to suggest that we go out for dinner at Pancho's, her favorite Mexican restaurant, only a few blocks away.

"With Molly?" I smile through my dread.

"Sure. Why not?"

"Won't she be ready for a feeding? Be cranky?" Horrifying memories of a wild, red-faced scene at a Love's barbecue, with three anxiety-ridden baby boys wailing amid pools of spilled milk and a broad scattering of French fries on the floor, hurdle a gulf of 18 years.

"I can always feed her."

"There?" I think breast-feeding is wise and wonderful and beautiful, but like a majority of my over-civilized brothers and sisters, I draw the line at it being done in public—particularly in a restaurant.

"Sure," says my little earth mother. "Well?"

"Well . . . I guess we can try it."

My tamale combination plate and Timarie's chicken taquitos are delicious. I know this because not three minutes into the eating of them Molly expresses herself with a loud and piercing hunger cry. While Pancho's is by no stretch of the mind a clone of Ma Maison, disturbed and disapproving heads do turn toward our booth.

"Let's change places," Timarie says softly. "I'm going to feed her."

I sheepishly do her bidding, and I see as I slide into her previous place across the table that she has already read the restaurant's seating placement, and that my previous position happens to be shielded from all young and middle-aged males' gazes...and most everyone else's, too. Once she delves into her nursing bra, blouse, sweater and blanket layers, nothing shows but the bobbing back of Molly's little red-fuzzed pate.

Throughout dinner I talk on as though nothing really out of the ordinary is happening, and most diners soon go back to their tacos and enchiladas and own conversations. An exception is the booth directly across from us, where an elderly gentleman and his wife and what appears to be their grown daughter have watched us, approvingly, and have asked questions about our baby.

At nursing's end Timarie holds Molly up in her full glory on the table top so they can look her over. Refreshed, Molly again shows her surprising strength by flexing her legs and springing upward in bursts of joyous energy, her blue eyes round as full moons, radiant with tomorrow.

Our dining companions heap compliments on her, and later when they are ready to pay their check and leave, the gentleman turns to us a last time and says, in a voice wise and civilized, "Thank you for sharing your little daughter with us."

What the hell do I know about civilization!

# July 4    *Parade*

Timarie is determined to enter community life on this special day devoted to honoring *liberté*. I kill the morning hour-and-a-half of diaper-changing and coffee-making and clothes-washing singing, not quite sotto voice, "I-I-I hate a parade...."

Huntington Beach, the former grimy oil town and long-time surfers' mecca, where twisted fate has cast us up as a family, lately has come into its own as a fast-prospering, semi-sophisticated Orange County community of 170,000. Ironically, it was the slow drying up of the extensive petroleum fields first tapped in the 1920s, and the gradual removal of unsightly rigs and tanks and pipes, that reserved open space for the present growth spurt, which is decidedly upscale and future-thinking. But today the city looks back with its traditional Fourth-of-July Parade, old hometown America shamelessly showing all on Main Street.

I stall, sip a Kirin, and hope Tim's habit of running behind schedule will get me out of it. Not to be. Timarie finally readies herself and Molly. "We can still catch the tail end," she says to me consolingly. Yeah. Great. Time to pack the car for a mile-drive to the parade route.

Small, small world indeed. In just a four-block walk we meet two mothers who were among the 15 or so couples in our natural childbirth classes. We exchange warm if superficial words of renewal, comparing labor ordeals, confirming exact birth times and weights, admiring each others' babies. The first is a gregarious Japanese-American school teacher who's living the same summer-at-home-with-baby life I am and his Irish-looking wife. They've wrought a truly beautiful, round-faced little girl who wears a big yellow sun hat for the parade. I wouldn't mind comparing notes with the guy, but they're in a hurry to get to grandma's.

The second mother is without spouse and at paradeside when we thread our way through the thinning crowd and unexpectedly sidle up next to her. She and Timarie exchange effusive greetings while I hang shyly back. Tim pulls Molly's sunbonnet back to exhibit my sleeping daughter to the other mother and a knot of admiring strangers. Their chatter becomes more animated as they get into the smarmy core of mothering. Time for me to get in some serious parade-watching.

A troop of Marines in dress blues marches by. "Those are the guys we should have sent in to handle Khomeini," the thirtyish guy at my left elbow says to a male companion. I squirm uncomfortably. Public displays of religion and nationalism always irritate me. Thankfully, the second fellow, balding and in shorts and tending a baby in a stroller, tactfully turns down the offer to add fuel to the patriotic fire.

I find additional relief and no little satisfaction in learning that some kindly entrepreneur has been considerate enough to sell hot and thirsty parade-watchers beers from his front lawn. I also discover that beer improves parade-watching immeasurably. The performing skills of the high school bands soar. The twiggy baton twirlers from the visiting Long Beach Girls' Club seem graceful buds about to bloom. Local politicians and business leaders, appropriately dressed as clowns, grant us smiles that tell us they are our good buddies.

I start warming to Orange County's America on its down-home toot. Then, virtually at parade's end, I see a sight that is simultaneously sad and comic and flat-out marvelous. The West Orange County Democratic Club is marching, all of three strong, carrying a banner urging that everyone register and vote—not exactly the advice that Chairman Kirk would have approved in this election year. Talk about courage! I begin to clap, loudly it would appear from the puzzled faces that turn my way. One of those is Timarie's; she thinks I'm applauding the Red, White and Blues, a truly ear-offending band of teen-age cacophonics just passing her. No, I correct her with a finger of solidarity pointed behind the band...at the few...the proud....

"Wasn't she disgusting?" Timarie asks as we walk back to the car.

It takes me a few questions to identify the she as the other mother Tim's been in rapt conversation with for the last half hour.

"Did you see what she was wearing?" "Yes." I wisely content myself with a one-word response. The woman had worn an undersized strapless top over ample, if rather slack, breasts. Eye-catching...not unpleasantly so.

"I think it was pretty cheesy."

Perhaps. Yet provocative, as all boobs are when they're not actually being used for what they're intended to be used for, at which time they become asexual, yet objects for study and wonder and respect for their place in our mammalian odyssey. I guess I've never seen a tit I didn't like.

"Why are you smiling?"

"Nothing."

"You thought the parade was corny, didn't you?"

"Hey! You think I'd knock Molly's hometown?"

# July 5     *"Louganis"*

Our daily walk, with Molly huddled down inside the Napsak and me sweating in my sweats, ends before Timarie awakes on this, one of her sleep-in Saturday mornings.

So Molly and I wake her and show her our new game, "Louganis." It's a dandy, not to mention it being a more demanding one for my growing Molly. Yes, she dives from the height of my extended arms into the mattress. No, she doesn't do any back flips or two-and-a-half gainers because there's no way I can turn my arms into pretzels. Actually, she prefers the straight-ahead swan dive, with me pulling her out of it just as she brushes the mattress. But she'll do a cutaway and a one-and-half twist, too, with some grimacing. Admittedly, the degree of difficulty may not be all that much, but she consistently scores 8.5s on my card. I should also admit that I'm fonder of this game than Molly is.

After her afternoon bath, Molly is placed between us on the bed by Timarie. The two of us flank her and watch her go through her leg-kicking and arm-thrashing exercises, as is our family custom. Suddenly, Molly rolls stoutly right from her back toward her stomach. Her right arm wedges between her right side and the mattress, preventing completion of the body flip. Molly begins an angry cry.

"You can do it!" Timarie shouts encouragingly. "You can do it!"

And she can! Rolls over the first time! Goes from back to stomach—the harder way!—before she's two months old. Who cares if it takes her a full four minutes of struggle, accompanied by an emotional progression of cries from irate to outraged, before she rips free her caught right elbow and completes the roll to Tim's cheers. Impressive feat. Nasty temper.

Of course she is a redhead. No way she got that trait from her Dad.

## July 6     *Designers Be Damned!*

**B**ought by adults who have never had a baby, designed by those who have never dressed a baby....

It's time to get this off my chest and put it on the record. The most exasperating moments—no, make that hours—with Molly are not, as one might imagine, quieting the crying, the endless wiping of the bottom or the frequent changes of shirts sopping with spit-up. It's putting on and taking off designer clothes, garments made by idiots who have no idea what a baby is built like. You practically have to break their arms or wring their necks to get them into the damn things. And then you always have to reverse the process when you take them off. More mutual pain.

Right on top of my offenders' list is Christian Dior. True, while on, and with the label cleverly exposed, the "outfits" may get you a lot of "how darlings!" and "how cutes" on your shopping expeditions (mostly from fashion-conscious barren women, methinks); it's just too bad the guy and his cohorts never actually saw a live human infant.

More and more I pass over these once-worn works of art when I dress Molly. I have my own list of wants. Start with the neck. Have it loose—maybe a V-neck—or with snaps, so that you don't suffocate the baby pulling the shirt over the head; the skull is the largest part of the infant's body, as is certainly fitting for a species that relies so heavily on the brain for survival. Avoid clothes with binding elastic in the arms or legs (or snip it when it starts leaving indentations in the skin); unrestricted circulation is as important for an infant as it is an adult. It's also wise to trim off inside threads and tags that irritate. Better, too, I think, to put them in drawstring nightgowns at night rather than sleepers; when you have to change them, you just open, diaper, and close, without the early-morning hassle of a partial disrobing. The same logic has me favoring snap-up tee-shirts over those you have to pull over their heads. I also prefer the outer garments with two or even three rows of snaps that allow you to adjust for length or girth as the baby grows...they're more comfortable on the child and they last longer, too.

As a general rule, I favor cotton (ideal for California summers) that is neither bouffant nor Speedo in the fit, but the perfect in-between. Pilucho—garments with a generous pelvic allowance and three adjustments in button snaps (significantly, from J. C. Penney)—is a brand I find sensible and Molly finds comfortable.

All this boils up today when I try to put Molly into a fancy Dior sunsuit—the gift of a well-meaning friend—for the first time. I wouldn't have tortured her with the try if I hadn't first discovered that my favorite little sleeper/creeper, white terrycloth with a little red bow up front, no longer comfortably fits and might conceivably compress her little spine. How quickly she grows. How fast the summer goes.

I should here add that Timarie does not agree with my "Theory of Designer Clothes." She suggests that my troubles spring from A) never playing with and therefore dressing dolls when I was small, and B) never being known for my manual dexterity.

Everyone is entitled to his or her own opinion, no matter how patently absurd it may be.

## July 7  *Crisis In The Food Supply*

We've seen the crisis coming. Since a week before Timarie went back to work she started pumping breast milk to build up a supply for those two feedings a workday we figured she'd miss with Molly. When she returned to the job she took her breast pump with her, intending to bottle the results during her lunch hour as a replacement for what's consumed at home. Sure sounded good on paper.

Trouble is, Timarie can't pump in one session as much as Molly and I use while she's gone. And doubling the trouble is that Molly now suddenly has decided to refuse her formula (the same stuff she so easily accepted and that sustained her during the breast-infection episodes). She squirms and forces the rubber nipple out of her mouth with her tongue. The lady's developed a taste, it seems, and we're running out of her brand.

At the 10:00-a.m. feeding I try five bottled ounces of Isomil. Two drops on her tongue and she spits it out and whips her head from side to side, then starts crying.

I'll wait her out. Hunger always breaks pride.

Not at 10:30. Again she refuses, though her hunger cries sharpen. At 10:50 a third try ends in failure.

Her wailing is sandpapering my nerve endings....I'm getting panicky. Do I continue until she just has to accept formula? At 11:00 a.m. I call Dr. Chang for advice, and luckily I get her.

"Do you have any breast milk left?" she asks.

"Yes, I've got six ounces in reserve." It's my ace in the hole—the ration that will keep Molly alive until she can be rushed to the hospital and fed intravenously.

"Then try cutting the formula, half-and-half."

My hands tremble as I measure the mix out against a background of non-stop crying—hunger crying—as if I needed the cutting edge and timbre to know that.

Back to the reclining chair. Cradle her in my left arm, until she's almost parallel to earth. Move the nipple to her lips. Hold my breath.

Her tongue flicks out and tests two drops on the nipple's end. Pulls back. I splash a little around her mouth. The tongue comes out for another stabbing try, starts to pull back as the head turns away. I follow with the nipple, jabbing her lips, getting a bare trickle into her mouth. She tastes it. I slip the nipple into her mouth. She heaves one sigh and latches on, the first three drafts reluctantly taken, but then with gathering gusto through the rest of the five ounces. Bravo!

At the 2:25-p.m. feeding there is no resistance at all to the half-and-half. Eureka! We've reached an accommodation and Molly will not waste away.

I like living with people who are willing to compromise.

## July 8     *Enduring Modesty*

I have to tend to some school business today, so I drop Molly off with Timarie's mother for a few hours. At school I run into a young female student who's taken three courses from me, and done well in them.

"How's the summer going?" she asks.

"Great," I respond con brio.

"How's the baby?"

"Really great."

She hesitates, awkward, something on her mind. "You're taking care of her?"

"Yes."

"Alone? You do everything?"

"Sure. Why not?"

Only after she blushes and turns her back to walk away do I realize what has flustered her. My answers imply that I'm changing her and bathing her and wiping her bottom and pudendum (how easily we seek refuge in Latinate words, fleeing their earthier Anglo-Saxon equivalents), and have otherwise entered into a private female realm.

Am I really so different in what I'm doing—playing masculine mother to Molly for one summer?

Already Kurt's friends refer to me as "Mr. Mom," after some movie they've seen, and exchange not-quite respectful grins.

What's this all about? Hasn't sex education in the schools made these young people more unisexual and less prudish, as I've read in the press?

Where are all these folks with healthy sexual attitudes? I keep reading and hearing about them, but I've still to meet one.

I'd like to stand tall on the subject. But the conversation fans a back-of-the-mind, low-grade worry that's been smoldering in this second-generation father. What if, by whatever circumstance, it fell to me to explain to Molly Margaret what my father called (without ever divulging) "the facts of life." Could I do it?

I take some modest pride in how I told my sons about sex, avoiding the errors of my prudish father. I gave it to them straight, stripped of any academic jargon or sex manual euphemisms, in the original English, the language they used and understood best. And they have since thanked me for telling them plainly how it all works, if not what it all means.

But could I do the same with Molly?

Timarie had better take good care of herself.

Though well-behaved at Margaret's, Molly is cranky when I get her home. Too much moving around? Coming down with a bug? Digestive trouble?

God! I wish I were smarter. Younger. Could remember things better. Here I've got this precious cargo in my charge and I'm frightened. Yes. I can tell that by the way my hands quake as I mix the milk that I hope will stop Molly's distress cries I hear coming from the master bedroom.

I've heard and read that these feelings of inadequacy come with being a new parent. Well, hell! I don't have that excuse. I raised three sons. Got them to their late teens alive and reasonably intact, which I'll take credit for, thank you!

Still, it doesn't help now. It's like starting over without a valid memory of the last time through this peculiarly long and convoluted series of complicated tasks we prime primates are cursed to learn. That's what gives me the shakes.

Yes. All true. Confession? I secretly enjoy living on this blade edge of life!

# July 9     *No Upchucks*

When I first thought of keeping this journal, I resolved to learn much and pass on the gold I'd mined to anyone who would read these pages. But I've botched it. Once more my reach has exceeded my grasp. I hardly have time to read the literature to see when Molly will be crawling.

One thing I *have* learned is that, for the new mother and the senior father, gold takes on a lesser value than breast milk. I learned that lesson last Sunday the hard way when I spilled an ounce in a bottle-to-bottle transfer and got a royal chewing out from the maker.

Another thing I have learned—this more satisfying to my ego—is to feed Molly so I don't get the massive upchucks her mother and various aunts get and complain of. I have learned to cradle her in my left arm, feed her precisely an ounce and a half rather rapidly, then walk her through the house, with her body vertical in a press against my chest, even if it takes five minutes, until that necessary burp comes. She might complain briefly at the hiatus in her dining, but not for long, because she seems to know what's expected. And she keeps down the nourishment.

How do I explain this success? I think when she's leisurely breast-feeding, the milk enters her mouth gradually and moves into her stomach slowly, so there's always something in the digestive canal to come back up even with delayed burping, whereas with my method the milk goes down "clunk" and has a too-steep vertical climb to come back up.

No, I can't support that with any citations in the medical literature. Just take it for what it is . . . a little practical wisdom from an old/new househusband.

## July 10     *When Buying A Car...*

Walking with Molly is fine, but it limits our range on days like today—days of many important errands. Mainly, we've got to get printing bids for business cards and stationery. I decide we'll scrap today's morning walk to conserve her energy (or is it really her patience?) and move her afternoon feeding up to 1:00 p.m. Then, still fresh and with full bellies, we'll invade the nearby world.

What a bloody bother it is to belt Molly into the infant seat, secure the seat in the car, tie the Napsak on my chest, drive to the destination, stop, unbelt Molly from the infant seat, arrange her in the Napsak, drop off my request for a bid over her flailing arms, walk back to the car, remove her from the Napsak, belt her into the infant seat, then drive to the next vendor and do the whole damn thing all over again. And yet we manage to go through three such calls over an hour and 15 minutes' time and 23 driving miles without complaint. Not so the fourth stop. No sooner do I state my wants to this genial printer, who tells me he's just had his first grandson, than Molly demonstrates her lung-power.

"I'll have to go. . .just mail me the bid, if you will," I ask, backing out of the shop toward my car.

"I will," he promises. "I'll get it out this afternoon." (A lie, by the way. He never did. Which is no surprise to those who have dealt with printers. The last one to tell the truth died in 1793, hanged by his fellow tradesmen for setting a dangerous precedent.)

As always, once underway in the car, Molly slips into a contented doze. As I approach a Chrysler-Plymouth dealership, I think, why not stop in briefly and check out the new Reliant, one of the candidates for replacing our two terminal clunkers, on this slow Thursday afternoon, when I can slink about the lot, unmolested, checking sticker prices?

Molly takes the transfer back into the Napsak without initial complaint. As I reach the lot and take my first peek inside a tan sedan, here he comes, all smiles, wearing a nicely cut vanilla-ice-cream-colored suit with faint-green-pin-striped shirt and raspberry-colored tie popped neatly out with a pearl stickpin.

"Got something particular in mind?"

"Just wanted to check out the leg room in the Reliant," I respond, hoping I'll get the chance to sit in the car without having to hear the pitch.

"Let me show you one on the other side of the lot... it's got bucket seats and would probably be better for...."

On that final word Molly's awakening anger masks all. The not-so-smiling fellow, probably one of those celebrated leopards of the singles' bars, backs off quickly, saying, I think, that I should come and get him if I see anything I like.

In the car again and Molly quiets. Why not try again? The Toyota dealer—his Tercel wagon is another candidate—is only a mile and a half from home and bottle and cradle....

It is a repeat of before. The switch to the Napsak is safely done, but as I approach the lot and the idle salesman approaches me, Molly vents her full frustration. The Toyota guy, dressed in a dark blue-and-white houndstooth jacket with razor-edged pressed gray slacks, is older... a family man, he claims as he backs off, but seemingly unwilling to relive the years of yore. "If you need any questions answered...."

I have the run of the lot, able to sit in any and all cars as Molly cries away in my lap.

For those of you who think this book's been a waste of money 'til now, here's my money-saving tip that will reward you with at least enough money to buy and send to friends—or foes—an additional 20 copies of this volume.

Pick the precise color and model of car, and the extras and add-ons, in advance. Make sure the kid is robbed of a feeding, and awakened prematurely from a nap, then drive directly to the new car dealer. There, brandishing the bawling babe, you say, "Take me to your closer—pronto!"

# July 11     *All In A Day's Domestication*

Perhaps it's my advancing age, or having a first daughter, or both, or more, but my domestication continues, seeming more natural than strange to me now. Is it that the nearness to the quiet hearth and the distance from the crowded marketplace turns one that way? Has this summer with Molly just turned me from a big wild-bull macho into a limp-wristed candy-assed wimp, as some male acquaintances seem to suggest in their gaping stares?

Today, after Molly bolts during a changing and drives an open safety pin into my thumb—my first such mishap on this round of generation—I cut loose with a leash of four-letter words. Immediately, I'm overcome with shame. Nobody uses that kind of language around my daughter!

This is to be a rough day in my summer with Molly. I'm out of sorts from filling out insurance forms and wasting other hours on stupid paperwork (yeah, paying bills) and then it's time to run the errands—to the bank, to the cleaners, the deli, the post office, a supermarket—with Molly in seeming endless shuffle between the infant seat and the Napsak, and back again, which interrupts her snoozes with necessary bumpings and bouncings.

When I drop my double coupons on the floor in Von's checkout line, I have to squat and gather them up with one hand while holding Molly parallel to the floor with the other, so she won't slip out of her sack. An elderly woman apologizes for not helping me pick them up. I tell her it's OK, that bending is good for me—it keeps me in shape. Fortunately, I've learned from my previous stint as a father to keep my left hand cupped behind the baby's head, so that the counter wall raps my knuckles, not her occiput.

Just as I straighten up and fish my checkbook out of the Napsak, Molly poops, audibly, sad to say. Since I'm wearing running shoes and can't do any noisy floor scraping to mask the sound, I ignore it, pretending as well that gas is not being passed.

When I stagger in with Molly and the groceries, Timarie is waiting.

"You left the milk out again."

"So I did. Sorry, I'm not Superman."

I reach for the Bloody Mary mix. "But I might be mistaken for his grandfather, on a good day."

# July 12 *Walkers And Gawkers*

Kurt's using my car to drive to work at a construction site in Long Beach. But it's OK.

Molly and I are into a walking rhythm now. She shrinks down into the Napsak before we're half a block from home and drops into a light sleep. I bump and jostle her as I quicken the pace to raise a sweat and shed some of the matronly pounds I've been picking up; periodically I open the top to check that her neck's not too badly bent and to kiss her on her red fuzztop.

We're becoming regular attractions at a few local supermarkets, the bank, the cleaners, and the post office. And gawkers have to earn their peeks. If they're genuinely nice and interested in my Celtic beauty with the red hair, the ultra-pale skin that reveals the blue rivulets of her veins; on special occasions, for special people, when I think it's worth it to wake her, I tease open her eyes, which are some days violet, some days Pacific blue, and most days an arresting blend between.

This evening, Molly, wearing her cutest smiling quizzical face with pouting bow mouth and roundest eyes, utters one-syllable sounds, trying to talk to me. Her fragility, my mortality, and the poignancy of the moment trigger a rush of deep and painful love I can only put into the words, tremulous in the exhale, "You're wonderful! You're wonderful!"

This is my second Chernobyl.

# July 13     *Her First Stroller Ride*

My pale Gaelic girl with the thin carrot top and violet-blue eyes is two months old today. To make a memorable day of it, Timarie dresses her up in what she knows to be my favorite undershirt—a white cotton double-breasted one with snaps (yeah! so you don't scare them breathless with an over-the-head pull) and a lavender heart cross-stitched on the left side by her Auntie Maggie, which I call her purple heart—and a pair of lavender rosebud panties and a matching sunbonnet.

We take pictures, and then Dad takes her on her first stroller ride, which sounds better in theory than works out in practice. First, Molly is just too small to sit upright in the seat, no matter how many pillows and receiving blankets are inserted as bumpers. Second, if you try to save her from the violent, neck-wrenching lurching of the moving stroller by lowering the seat into the ground-parallel position, then the bright unshaded sun all but blinds her. Third, the sidewalk pavement blocks are jarringly uneven, as one learns to accept in time in earthquake country; Molly, of course, hasn't had enough time. Finally, our house is a short three miles from the Pacific, and the stiff afternoon breeze we have come to love for its refreshing wafts in summer pleases Molly not...unless they're zephyrs at her back.

I return a tired and unhappy girl to the house after our abbreviated spin in the Strolee. And she spends the afternoon spitting-up more than usual.

The wind wanes with nightfall, and Timarie takes Molly onto the patio to check the evening sky. The baby stares out at the first evening stars with her brow knitted in apparent thought.

"What do you think she's doing?" Timarie asks me.

"She's looking into her future."

"What does she see?"

"Herself as one of the great women of history," I blurt, wanting as quickly to retrieve the words; I have a low opinion of parents who set marks for their children they themselves have never reached, then not-very-subtly apply pressure in that direction.

"That's after she's potty-trained, right?"

Right.

# July 14  *The Fine Art Of Finessing*

Tim takes her car to work, Kurt takes my car to work, so I am left without wheels again, barefoot, and I might as well be pregnant for all the mobility I have. And yet, today at least, being house-bound with changing diapers and warming bottles doesn't bother me at all. Could I be developing agoraphobia? Me? One who, by fate, if not actual disposition has been a rootless sort, with 44 residences in 53 years, is suddenly finding the sedentary life agreeable? Well, yes, for the time being.

It's well after our dinner, and Timarie has settled into the leather recliner chair, her "nursing station," as she calls it, next to a table that bears a log of Molly's feedings, baby readings, and the phone. But I notice the usual seraphic expression is missing on the mother.
"What's wrong?"
"Nothing," she says, unconvincingly.
"Come on...tell me what it is."
That's all the coaxing she needs. Out it pours—her anger when a friend raised her brows disapprovingly that day upon hearing that Timarie was drinking a daily beer while nursing Molly.
"I told her that even Dr. Chang recommended it, but I don't think she believed me."
"You should have added that the beer was Kirin Draft...nobody should be denied that," I say lightly.
Not funny. Tim's in that never-never land of feeling half-wronged and half-guilty, and is in no mood for banter.
"Hey! You're right and so is Dr. Chang. Beer in moderation is good for lactating mothers...that's ancient wisdom—even I know that." I go on to tell her about my sainted mother, a saloon keeper's daughter but also a teetotaler—except when she was breast-feeding her four children, and then she forced herself to drink the bitter brew, and swore by its milk-producing powers.
Timarie smiles. She's convinced...and Molly's asleep. "Would you 'finesse' her?" she asks.
I stand. I am being called on to perform a skill I've honed over the last month. I move stealthily over to the sleeping girl, gently slip my open

right palm under her midsection, then even more gently lift her until she is in the attitude of an airplane in level flight, but with its wings dangling limply. I provide the power—quick and silent—by gliding in level movement up the hall toward her cradle, left hand a shield for her fragile head. In one easy motion I set her softly face down on her sheet and silently fold the blanket up around her. Without her ever waking. At least nine out of ten times I pull it off, which makes me an acknowledged "master of finesse." At least around this house.

## July 15     *Many Errand Day*

We are going to stretch today—Molly and me. Get our walk and morning nap out of the way early and then, since I have my car again, drive about towns (in over-settled Southern California there are no discernible boundaries between communities) on our many errands.

The bank's a breeze. Molly remains asleep when the friendly teller asks if she can see her and I proudly unzip the Napsak.

Since she's asleep, I leave her in the infant seat for our visit to the post office, which always has a long line. Today is no different, and though we draw many stares and a few thoughtful inquiries as to her age, Molly slumbers on, even when I reach the window and have to put her on the floor between my feet while I conduct business.

At the cleaners I keep her in the infant seat rather than disturb her sleep, but the banging around she gets when I try to carry both her and the cleaned-and-pressed suit and sweaters isn't worth it.

At the computer store, where I've dropped in to see the new Leading Edge Model D package, Molly starts twisting and turning in her sack and making little sounds of irritation that the salesman must adjust his sales spiel around. "I'll be back to talk some more," I tell him after I gather up the sales brochures. He opens the door for me.

There's major agitation in the bag as I enter the telephone repair store with my busted phone in hand. Two other customers are awaiting service and one of them is loudly berating the guy behind the counter for his incompetence. Loudly, however, must make way for louder this afternoon. Molly cuts loose with her loudest-ever bawl of protest. Conversation ends. Heads turn. I do an about-face and scoot out the door.

In the car I look at my watch: 4:09 p.m. I have committed the folly of being out and about at the children's hour, which, as all parents know, is really two hours—from 4::00 to 6:00 p.m.—and for which there is no known remedy.

When I had my first family I thought these afternoon storm-and-tantrum sessions might be displays of sympathy for my having to drive the crowded freeways. But I have subsequently found in the literature that the phenomenon existed before Los Angeles had freeways—even before there were automobiles.

# July 16     *Words, Words, Wonderful Words*

**M**obile-mawed Molly Margaret's mouth moves to the sounds I make, nonsense sounds she seems to try to imitate, puts on antic masks I wear, and earns the state of joy that awaits the willing fool.

Good golly, Miss Molly... you're too good to be true, says I to her, to split a pop-music allusion.

Late in the afternoon, while changing Molly, I notice for the first time a second birthmark—this this one small, perhaps three-centimeters square, a slightly reddened patch, just above her left elbow, on the outside. Is it new? Has it been there all along? Anyway, will it go away? I will have to ask Dr. Chang. I'd prefer no disfigurements at all on my angel girl.

## July 17     *Dollar Days*

Today I must drop Molly at her grandmother's for an hour while I go to the dermatologist. I'm paying the price of many a California boy who lived too many summers with my shirt off. I have some patchy changes in skin color, including a rough reddish raised area on my left arm the size of a pinkie nail. I am worried.

The doctor, a bright, hyperenergized guy just entering midlife, asks me about my new daughter as he checks the spot out.

"The greatest thing that ever happened to me," I tell him as he burns the thing off with his electric scalpel.

He's divined my concern. "Of course, I'll send it out for biopsy, but I'm all but sure it's nothing worse than pre-cancerous. You'll live to dance at your daughter's wedding."

It was a nice thing to say, I think as I pay the bill, but I sure wish I had it in writing.

"I'm taking the checkbook, and I'm gonna spend a lot of money," Timarie says as soon as dinner's over.

"I'm not worried about that," I say, kissing Molly's head as Mom packs the lavender diaper bag. "Molly won't let you stay long enough to spend much money, right Moll?"

I'm off to Los Alamitos and the horseraces with Rod for the shank of the night. I drop a modest ten dollars for the eight races we stay for; Rod does a little better.

When I get home at 10:56 p.m., Timarie and Molly have just pulled in. Timarie shows me the night's purchases.

I nod in feigned appreciation. Then I stand Molly on my stomach and bring her nose down to touch mine. "I was counting on you not to let her spend money. What happened? Huh? What happened?"

Molly smiles.

A conspiracy? Is America a moiety of shoppers and outnumbered skinflints?

## July 18  *Failed Promises*

This mid-morning, as I crook Molly in my arm and give her six ounces of formula-mother's-milk mix, I see her in all her delicacy. I call it that in rebellion against sensitivity, which is probably the better word. She is so pink in every way that I decide to call her Pinkerton. I say it over and over, as though I'm transmitting music to her. I build on that with butchered bits of nursery rhymes.

No, I realize I'm not living up to my promise—to those goals I set when I first planned this journal. I was going to research the subject of child rearing, consult doctors on the phone, interview experts in the field—dig out the fine points of pediatrics and pass them along to you.

I'm sure the mothers and fathers among you are not surprised that I barely have time to call doctors during those rare moments I can get to the phone between diaper-changing, feeding, burping, bottom-washing and walking the floor with a wailing infant. My apologies. Again, my reach has exceeded my grasp.

But would I change things if I could? Go back a year and call it all off? No way. One look at Molly, drowsy in the crook of my arm, tells me that.

Is it narcissistic to admit she fills my life? In her delicacy I see the remnants of my own sensitivity. And I want to pass to her things I know or am . . . my love of words most of all. So I recite verse fragments to her, sing nonsense songs to her, hoping the synergy of words and music will help fill voids for her one day.

# July 19  *Painting Walls And Painted Ladies*

This day I paint the living room and hall walls in the faint pink latex semi-gloss Timarie has chosen to complement the gray carpet and the antiqued burgundy leather sofa and chair yet to be delivered. Exhausting. Kurt's working at the market most of the day, so I don't have him to help me. And Timarie has taken Molly to her mother's while she gets her hair done.

By six I'm a sweat-sodden heap, done with the painting, but wasted, when Timarie walks in with Molly and a nervous smile on her face. I only have to wonder why for an instant. The reason is as plain as the hair on her head.

I know I will never understand the Byzantine relationship between a woman and her hair and her man. I really hope to get Einstein's general theory of relativity down first; even though it leads to such dubious gifts as nuclear fission and fusion, I know it will be safer in the long run.

"How do you like it?"

"Like what?"

"My hair!" A quaver of apprehension in the words.

"It's rather short."

"Yes, Jack just went wild... do you like it?" Enter paradox, which, in this instance leads inexorably to the end of the shooting gallery where the ducks pass in review. Timarie knows that I, like most American men (men the world over, probably), prefer long hair to short hair on a woman. Therefore, any *honest* answer I give must carry the clear message that *I prefer the long hair you had before to the short hair you have now.*

"How much did it cost?"

"Oh God! I just *couldn't* tell you that!"

"Is it supposed to be red?" I make passing mental note that the mother is building a cosmetic bridge to her daughter; I am not softened the way I should be.

"Well, I'm not real happy with the way it turned out."

"You're not?"

"No, Jack painted it and it's looking a little more blond than I thought it would... I may have him re-do it." (The mind wonders whether this "re-do" of a botched job will bring an additional charge. Under no circumstances will it bring back the shorn hair, you can be sure.)

"What *did* it cost?"

Agitated and sheepish at the same time. "I can't...."

"More than a hundred?"

The nod is in the affirmative. The paint fumes have left me nauseous.

"I'm going to kiss Molly," I say heading for the cradle.

"Wait! You haven't said anything about my hair....Do you like it?"

"Sure...if you're trying to look like a Paris tart on the prowl!"

No, I should not have said it, I know. But, you see, I'm trapped in the role of protagonist in a Greek tragedy, and I keep doing these same stupid things over and over, even though I know it's going to come out bad.

The emotional explosion registers in the 20-kiloton range, and as the dark postnuclear night comes to chilly close, I am found guilty of calling my wife a French whore.

Oh, Lord, stuck in Lodi again!

## July 20     *Family Funk*

The whole family dives into the funk today. Not much to say on this pleasant summer Sunday, which in California does not differ from most other Sundays.

Molly comes out of hers late in the afternoon, as I'm bouncing her on my chest. Her eyes are fixed, her mouth is formed in a lower-case "o" of wonder. What has captured her attention is the front of my tee-shirt, which reads, "Visit the Triassic/Petrified National Forest," along with a depiction of some pre-saurian thecodonts in an unlikely parade across my chest.

She studies it as she has not the previous tee-shirt, the one she barfed on, the one that read "Santa Anita/the Great Race Place," with four thoroughbreds in full run.

There are the same number of words on each, and the animal drawings on both are roughly equivalent in size and detail. May I extrapolate my daughter's future preference for paleontology over playing the ponies?

No, there is that simpler explanation. The Santa Anita letters and images are in orange and royal blue. The Petrified Forest and its fossil herd are black on white. As our infant-stimulation-class teacher told us, newborns prefer contrasting blacks on whites to colors. They really do.

# July 21     *It Tolls For Thee*

Ever wake up feeling sorry for yourself and wham!—you get shamed right out of it? That just happened to me. Molly woke at 6:13 a.m. for her dawn feeding, and, as Timarie took her to the breast, I went outside and got the *Times*. For no good reason I tossed the favored front page and the sports section on the bed between us and went first to the Orange County local news. The lead story's headline came and stuck me like a stiff left jab:

TWIN BABIES DIE UNATTENDED IN
CLOSED CAR; MOTHER, 25, HELD

I race through the story with a morbidity I despise in others, more agitated as I go. Yesterday afternoon three-month-old cross-twins were left in the back seat of an old two-door Chevy parked in the sun with one window cracked about an inch. The young mother went inside a store, apparently to visit a boyfriend, and then—it's unclear how much time elapsed—the mother returned to find the infants not breathing; they were rushed to a nearby medical center, where they were pronounced dead-on-arrival shortly after 12:30 p.m.

Three miles from where I lie! How could it happen? The temperature was only 78 degrees at noon! Yes, but Southern California heats-up quickly inside a stationary car, and the babies' immature cooling systems just weren't enough.

I tilt the newspaper away from Timarie's eyes so she won't see the story, though I know she'll find it soon enough. A deep two-column photo shows the grieving young mother with her arm and hand supporting a bowed head, slumping against the offending auto, its right front door now—belatedly—cracked open. The poor young woman! Why are they holding her? In a separate photograph the boyfriend is pictured sitting on the sidewalk, his head buried in his hands. How can fault be found where I see only victims?

Of course I see victims because the tragedy, or one similar, is for me personally as possible as tomorrow, as close as the nearest street. And like other parents who have newly given hostages to fortune, the fear is always there, like a raised knife....What if we lost our baby? Or a child? Losing a parent or a brother or sister—or even a spouse—is devastating enough...but what of losing a life unlived? Scarcely begun? And all because we didn't see death skulking among us, as it always is in one of its boundless disguises.

"I just couldn't go on," we say in horror at the thought. And we are comforted, just as we comfort others, with the words, "Yes, you would....It's difficult, but you do...you have to."

I suppose. But surely at some cost. "Any man's death diminishes me," John Donne wrote, "because I am involved in mankind." I don't think you have to be a world-class humanist to be diminished by the death of others—and especially your own child's. Isn't that the way it is? We existentialists begin by avoiding death, go on to protest against it, learn to hate it, even—if we are very proud—defy it. Yet by attrition, through mere exposure to it, death wears us down. Some it wins over. Most become inured to it and cease at end of day to rage against the dying of the light.

During this downer day I check on sleeping Molly's breathing six times.

## July 22     *Recipe For A Baby Bath*

**N**ervous time....Molly is due a one-on-one bath, and I can't dodge this one. Until now I've served several times as standby assistant, but this is my first time alone, and most of my morning is ruined with apprehension.

Molly is so small, and, when soaped, so slippery...and I have never been blessed with great hands. Truth is, I've been called clumsy more than once. An oaf, too, at least once.

It's 1:12 p.m. Lunch has been digested. We are both reasonably calm. Time to begin....

Draw the slightly less-than-lukewarm water in the bathroom washbasin. Put in the large yellow sponge in the general shape of a baby, with a recessed outline more clearly resembling a baby. Make sure the water level is at half-mast—enough to rinse her properly, and not so full that her head would go under if she slipped out of my hands; there would be enough time to grab her.

Now undress her on the bed and take her into the bathroom. Ease her gently, with the hands firmly under her arms, into the basin, being careful not to strike the chrome faucet, around which you've wrapped a washcloth buffer. (She's clean. Why am I bathing her?) Molly stares at herself in the mirror, her body relaxing in the familiar aquatic warmth.

With a soft washcloth and a little lather from the Dove soap, wash her chest (the right hand moves in two or three somewhat concentric circles and covers all, while the left spans her shoulders firmly), go down and get her thighs (right and then left, a stroke down and a stroke up); while you're at it lift her almost out of the tub with the left arm girdling her chest (some slight slippage there to quicken the heartbeat)—so you can run the washcloth down and around the tiny circumferences of her lower legs on this, the pre-rinse phase. Molly opens her mouth, but makes no sound.

Draw a deep breath. Relax. Now turn her around...so the span of your left hand cradles her chest. Then do the back, and the back of the neck (a little something there in the creases—probably puke), then down the cutest bottom ever and onto the thighs, past the little bar-shaped birthmark, and down for the merest suggestion of a brush at the heels. Molly's mouth is open in the smile configuration.

Exhale whatever you've got; get ready for the hardest part, which comes last...probably shouldn't have come last, come to think of it, but actually first, and I've probably reversed the proper order...or at least the Japanese, civilized lovers of the bath that they be, would think so, because no one washes the face and hair in what has already been used for allegedly inferior parts of the human anatomy.

Yep, the depressions on the face are lightly scrubbed, the fine red head hair rubbed back into carrot-gold whorls and spit-curls. (Your boys hated this part...remember how they thrashed around in your hold?) Molly hates it, too... but she doesn't thrash so much...because she's a girl? But Molly cries, exuberantly.

Now for the trickiest maneuver...reach over with the right hand for the hooded terrycloth towel and bring it in as you lift her from the tub, then slip the hood part over the back of her head (a halting action when wet skin meets dry towel), while replacing—with a heart-fluttering split-second of no-support—the left hand that's been bracing Molly's head and neck with the right hand.

Bring her to you, so her uncovered front is not exposed to the air (they can't maintain body heat as well as we), then walk carefully but quickly to the bed, gently set her down on it face to you and immediately rub—gently always—the beads of water off her front as you smile and baby-talk your head off. She smiles...chest heaves...smiles some more...goes slack...eyelids droop on the way to drowsiness. Swab out her ears with a Q-tip while you've got her in a good mood.

Yes, Molly likes her bath—a hell of a lot more than I like giving it to her.

Maybe that's not the best way to give an infant a bath. But that is the way I soloed this warm July day on planet earth, orbiting a modest-sized star said to be the property of the Milky Way galaxy.

# July 23     *Nature Over Nurture*

Molly is manic today, gone wildly flailingly kinetic after an enormous bowel movement at 11:07 a.m. The golden explosion gilded her legs, soiled her parents' bedsheet, and stained my priceless (it actually was a premium give-away, but I lost $54 that day) Santa Anita/the Great Race Place tee-shirt...it'll need Biz at least. Yet she smiles on in relief, as long as I give her my total, undivided attention, as they say. But she's angry and jarringly loud in her cries when I turn my head and try to do something else...like mix and warm her feeding.

Mood swings run low and high and sudden on her father's side of the family tree...may she be blessed with more ups than downs. From her mother she gets calm and early wisdom, directly. What a formidable blend she could be! *Sturm and drang* and cerebral drive with optimism and a compassionate understanding of the real and the possible. For my Molly, Katie (or Katrina) bar the door!

# July 24      *Fed Up And Far Behind*

This falling behind is getting to me. The house looks and smells like Tamerlane and his horde stabled their horses in it for a week, Molly is constantly fussing, and I can't find a damn thing I need—including overdue doctors' bills and insurance premiums in all this truck. I can't even get to the Kaypro...so even these complaints have to be scribbled out on scraps of paper I hope I'll be able to find later.

Molly has chosen this day to do a first-rate puke-out on the new carpet as I walk her and burp her. She leaves a trail of gray spots impervious to my sponge-dabbing, spots that intersperse in a suggestion of regularity with the Woolite Rug cleaner-resistant food stains, the asphaltum deposits from Kurt's boots, terminal Prunella's blood spatters, etcetera. Yeah, it was the wrong choice of carpet color. Nice going, Lare!

Timarie calls. She and the girls are having a happy hour today—business variety. She'll be by before 6:00 p.m. to pick up Molly, whom she wants to show off in her pink-hooded sweatsuit and tiny white sneakers banded with red stripes. Then Mother and Daughter will proceed on to South Coast Plaza with friend Mary and her daughter, Whitney, for some shopping...to buy...? I forget.

There's always something to buy in your modern major mall in the land of the free and the home of the brave and the haunt of the conspicuous consumer, properly armed with plastic.... Especially in Orange County, California.

And yet, I relish this rare time at the word processor, by myself for a change, where I can try, over my fatigue, to get some of my feelings down. Most of them have to do with my resentment of Timarie and fear for them both as 10:00 p.m. comes and goes and they're still not home. The stores close at 9:00 p.m. The car she's driving is a clunking bomb waiting to explode with my precious double cargo.

At 10:20 p.m. Timarie returns, all smiles, with a sleeping Molly, whom she pronounces "perfect" in her behavior on this not-so-profitable shopping excursion.

"But the stores closed at nine, didn't they?" says I, from bed.

"Yes. Mary and I decided to have a snack, the babies were so well behaved."

It's irrefutable logic, for one as tired as I. But I'm hardly mollified.

# July 25     *Blow-Up*

Things start falling apart right away.

Before work, Timarie goes back to Jack for a patch-up. I have consulted the checkbook and found that the first butchering cost $133—an amount that would see me through ten months of haircuts.

When she returns in the late morning her hair is further cut, to a conservative boy's length. "With the baby and all the demands, it's easier to manage this short," she says by way of explanation, or defense.

I resist the desire to know if Jack slashed her purse—*our* purse—again as well. "I think it's time we had a talk. A serious talk. I've got some complaints to put on the table." My tone is grave.

Timarie says she does, too, almost testily. Agreed, then. Tonight after dinner, over a glass of wine, perhaps, we will discuss our mutual dissatisfaction in a rational, forthright and constructive manner.

I spend the day between Molly's feedings and changings and entertainings taking notes, dredging up—and it doesn't take much dredging, because I am one of those rats who never forgets a slight—what dirt's been done me.

Tim returns at 6:00 p.m., grim-miened as I rarely see her, fortunately. We eat the baked red snapper, boiled new potatoes and green salad in a clumsy near-silence. The glass of wine for later becomes the entire bottle now. . . to ease the ways for ships that must clash in the night, we seem to agree without saying so.

I clear the dishes, Tim puts Molly down for what we hope is the final time, then we meet in the living room and take facing chairs for this very necessary if not inevitable "airing of differences."

OK, so I lied. I'm not going to make a clean breast of everything—particularly what was said over the next two and half hours. If I did, you'd say I sounded like a soap-opera composite of every wronged hausfrau who was ever left home barefoot and pregnant. True enough.

I do owe you, however, an abstract of my three major complaints in support of my case:

A. I am doing almost all the dishes. (My most legitimate beef—Tim and Kurt can, quite simply, outlast me when it comes to allowing pans and dishes to rise in irregular spires from the double sink and grow previously unknown microbial species.)

B. It is imperative that we sit down and put together a budget we can and will live by.

C. Finally, "Molly gets more of you than I do." (Right! The trump-card accusation of spousal-neglect! Yes, it can be dealt to stay-at-home husband-fathers, too.)

Our deliberations also come up with three mutually agreed-upon resolutions which might be worth imparting to mute a domestic flap or two:

A. We jointly resolve to level with each other instantly and in a positive way, and not let fancied slights burrow and grow into underground grudges.

B. We jointly resolve that the commitments one makes to the other be made within a time frame. That is, if you say you're going to do something, you also say when it's going to be done by.

C. We jointly resolve to pick up after ourselves, so our domicile will not continue to look like a Third World country.

# July 26    *Life On A Yo-Yo*

Wounds have been healed the old-fashioned way...with love. Great for greeting this new day, which is a special day. The chairman of my department is having a pool party this afternoon and Molly will make her social debut, lovingly dressed by her mother in a fetching pink sunsuit. I mean to show off to my skeptical colleagues that there's more to academic life than politics, tenure and sports. You can also marry a coed and start a new family.

The best laid plans go agley. As I bend to load the hatchback with the car-bed and diaper bag in one arm and Molly in the other, I feel a sharp pain in my hip and lower back. It persists and spreads as I limp back inside with Molly and the gear. I try some Tylenol. No relief. Aspirin and its kin have never worked for me. I pour a vodka. Then another. The pain gets worse until the least hurtful position I can find is prone on the rug, on my right side without moving a muscle. The party's off.

I turn on the tube for some sports dope to get through the afternoon and early evening.

By finger-poking I locate the two centers of pain. The major one is on the pelvic bone about an inch to the right of my coccyx; the second is the right hip's wing point. Both feel like an angry fire burns inside. So this is my payoff for all those games of Ripcord and Ferris Wheel and Moonwalk?

Maybe the whole thing was a mistake.

My gloom spreads to Timarie. "Do you think I'm good for you?" she asks, a question obviously formed out of some unpleasant residue from last night's conversation.

"Yes. You're leavening for my sour, yeasty Teutonic brew."

"That's a compliment?"

"Yes, and probably a scrambled metaphor, as well. I'm too bushed to think about it. Let's go to bed."

## July 27  *Self-Pity And Indignation*

We put Molly in the walker for the first time. It's supposed to be for infants in the six-to-nine-month range, but Molly's restless, and she also has long legs, which she extends to the fullest—just toe-touching the linoleum floor of the study. From in front of the Kaypro I watch her struggle with Graco's Tot Wheels II; the thing moves by accident, not intent, when it moves at all, the result of frustrated Molly putting down her foot in anger. She can't figure out what's disrupting her equilibrium, so the angrier she gets the more it moves and the angrier she gets—a vicious circle that might amuse me on a better day.

Poor thing! Poor me, too....My swivel chair also scoots around on wheels. What hurts is to know that one day soon Molly will master her walker and agilely move around at will. While I go the other way—into fast or slow decline...maybe in need of a walker myself before I know it. Self-pity is a terrible thing to waste, so I immerse myself in it on this nothing Sunday, redeemed only by Timarie's enduring optimism and Molly's smiles.

Yeats raised it all to lordly rage when he complained of being "fastened to a dying animal." Maybe I ought to pull down his little book. Read "Sailing to Byzantium" for starters, and really wallow in it.

# July 28     *As Long As You've Got Your Health*

The pain is not much better when I awake, so I beg an appointment with an orthopedist, this afternoon. Unfortunately, the only time I can get is 3:00 p.m., and Molly's scheduled visit to the pediatrician is at 4:00 p.m. So I will leave Molly in the care of Jean, the woman next door, at 2:45, Timarie will leave work early and pick her up there at 3:30 and take her on to Dr. Chang, and then after my visit is over, providing I'm ambulatory, of course, I will join them both.

The young orthopedist, Dr. Steven Graboff, takes notes as I describe my aches and pains. He asks if I've been doing any unusual physical activity. I tell him that, yes, I have a ten-pound daughter I lift often every day, and that I carry her in a pouch on my daily walks that range up to three-miles long. I also tell him I used to have a 20-minute daily regimen that included sit-ups and exercises with a Bullworker, but I just can't find the time for it anymore on a consistent basis.

"Let's take a picture," he says. I follow him to the X-ray room, get zapped from three angles, then am led back to his office, where I lapse into my usual brooding worry, when I think of all the good things I meant to do on earth but just never got to.

Dr. Graboff returns and takes a seat five feet away. He hesitates. My breath goes on hold. "There is nothing catastrophically wrong—nothing that will change your life overnight," he says. Not a hip dislocated . . . not bone cancer. Good. I'm over the big bumps. I'm feeling grateful and better already.

"The X-rays do show some micro-motion in the hip and some resulting inflammation . . . you've got arthritis there."

No surprise. I've already got it in my cervical vertebrae. Both should go well with the gout in my right knee and left elbow.

"The constant grinding there may have reached a nerve. . . .There's not much treatment for it. I will prescribe something for the painful episodes, though."

"Anything I can do in the way of diet—eat, not eat?"

"Take calcium, that's all. Calcium loss from the spine is common with this condition."

My next question is one I'm dreading the answer to. "Does this mean

I'll have to cut out my walks with my baby daughter?" (I've already added ten ill-placed pounds this summer from my reduced activity.)

"Where do you carry her?"

"Up-front, against my chest."

He smiles. "You can walk your daughter as much as you want. It's reaching out for things, lifting things off-balance that you want to avoid."

My mood is on the rise when I join Tim and Molly at the pediatrician's office, just as Molly's examination is about to begin. It continues up as Dr. Chang checks Molly out, verbalizing a chain of "goods" and "fines" as she pokes and peers. Molly is her curious jungfrau self, taking it all in, staring with her furrowed brow at the doctor.

"What an alert baby!" Dr. Chang says, seemingly to herself.

New parents devour such crumbs from their pediatricians. And having tasted them once, they hunger for more.

This night, as Timarie and I are about to doze off, I tell her that I have a title for her book.

"My autobiography?" she asks.

"Yes. *I Married a Geezer*."

# July 29    *A Small World After All*

Tim and Kurt have the autos again, and I am left carless and arthritic. Not much percentage in this gloom, though. Arthritis, be not proud. Molly and I will walk today.

A *pied* the world shrinks to what at first seems greater manageability. Probably more tiring and stifling, too, for the Southern Californian permanently without wheels. Such are my thoughts as I walk some morning errands. Molly is napping in the Napsak again, dreaming in the conducive California summer sunshine.

I've become keen on studying, sorting and quantifying the reactions I get from passers-by who realize that a tall man in his fifties and dressed in a sweat suit is, for some queer reason, carrying a very young infant in a frontal pouch, and often can be seen bending his graying head to impulsively kiss the exposed crown of its red head.

A simple majority refuses to allow itself to be seen seeing. About half the women above 25 years old smile or speak and say something nice.

With the men, a clear majority try not to see us at all. Only about 40 percent indicate they even notice the two of us, and maybe a third of them react. Two thirds of that third give me an incredulous stare, as though I were some raving nutball staggering over the buckled pavement tiles with my fly wide open. But that final third of the last two thirds—they're my soul buddies. Almost all guys over 50, they size-up what's going down and what a good deal I've got. "Nice going." "Atta Boy!" "Way to go!"

I'm ruminating on all this as Molly and I return from depositing $283 in the local Bank of America branch when it occurs to me that I haven't singled out young people, as I should, because that's what's surprising and sadly revealing. While some young women, judging from their smiles, clearly approve of my tending baby, as many—for whatever reason—register a chilly disapproval.

The dudes are even colder. They look at me like I'm some loony loose on their streets...scarcely worth stomping. One exception this day, though. In the last crosswalk crossing before we're home, a Datsun-ful of Southeast Asian teenagers brake their wagon. They smile and cheer as I cross in front of them. They understand....I guess....If they're sincere....Are teenagers ever sincere? Are they only insincere? Are they either? Don't ask me. I only raised three of them.

## July 30 *Goodbye Swyngomatic*

Alas! Swyngomatic has gradually lost its magic. Its former power to occupy Molly's mind and satisfy her love of rhythmic movement and just plain put her to sleep is no more. She cries and complains in it after the first few minutes now, unless I stick around to sing and dance and mug in front of her.

I should be pleased that the same old thing has become boring to her. But I'm not because I don't yet have a substitute. The blanket-on-the-floor-surrounded-by-toys gambit won't work yet because she's not strong enough to hold her head up for very long. And she's still too short to reach the floor and propel her Tot Wheels II walker around, even when it's adjusted to the closest-to-the-floor station.

There's another reason I can't rely on the Swyngomatic for anything but the slow-turtle setting any more. For weeks she's delighted in throwing her arms akimbo, and today I see that they now strike the device's four supporting struts if she goes very far forward or backward.

Yes, as others have observed, Molly has inherited my gibbon's-length arms. Fortunately, on her they look lovely, graceful in their long fluid sweeps. All they ever did for me was give some additional leverage and added pop to my fastball in those late years of my boyhood when I pitched baseballs... and later made those affordable off-the-rack suits and long-sleeved shirts of no use to me.

Consolation? Girls' clothes probably come in more variety.

# July 31     *Queen Upchuck*

Molly lived up to her title of Spit-Up Queen with some world-class barfing this morning, befouling two of my tee-shirts and two pairs of pants. She is no respecter of place, person or institution. UCLA, the Petrified Forest, Vivaldi at Lincoln Center and Santa Anita/The Great Race Place—all have now been subjected to the insult of her frothy spume.

That said, those uninformed acquaintances of Tim's who refer to it as "projectile vomiting" don't know what they're talking about. I do. My son Karl started projectile vomiting in his fifth week of life, and it was as though the mother's milk were shot out of his mouth through a hose nozzle's smallest aperture. At six weeks he underwent abdominal surgery for his pyloric stenosis.

That was my most worrisome time as a concerned father—watching the eight-pound little guy with his miniscule blood supply, and hooked-up to an I.V., being wheeled into an operating room for the big knife.

I am everlastingly thankful the too-thick muscle that walled the small intestine from the stomach was successfully cut down to size, and Karl today is a tall, strong, healthy young man.

No, Molly does not projectile vomit. But there's no doubt that she regurgitates to the max. And despite the pediatrician's and other mothers' claims that it's natural, I'm concerned about the loss of nourishment.

Or am I just picking that concern up from Timarie, who watches Molly's weight more closely than her own?

To reassure myself, I consult the doctor's weighing slips and, calculator in hand, find Molly's weight gain to average out at one ounce a day. Why, in ten years she'll weigh 228 pounds! Is that seeing the glass half-full or half-empty?

# August 1     *Blessed Are The Peacemakers*

Today we walk to my favorite Italian deli, which offers on Fridays three pre-mixed pizza doughs at the can't-beat price of 99 cents. I used to be a regular, but three months back I had a run-in with the head checker, who happens to be the owner's wife as well. I'd picked up some pecan rolls from the marked-down table that bore the numbers 109, which I assumed to be the price $1.09. No, it was a code for the employees, the checker curtly informed me in front of four queued customers.

"They look like a price to me," I grumbled, feeling I was being showed up.

"They are *not* a price, they are an employee code." Crisply and gratuitously delivered.

"Then keep your pecan rolls." I pushed them to her side of the counter.

Thereafter, when I did shop the deli, I made a point of going through the other check-out stand. If only the dragon lady had the duty, then our transaction would be quick, silent and tense.

This first day of August is one of those dragon-lady-only times.

I drop my three pizza doughs on the counter. The woman looks up, but not to the level of my eyes. She peers into the Napsak on my chest. "Red hair," she says softly, breaking three months of silence.

I seize the peace-making gesture. "Yes, and blue eyes, too," I say, proudly unzipping the bag so Molly, who has just surfaced from a nap, faces her.

The woman's smile is the broadest I've seen. "You have a beautiful daughter," she says.

"Thank you." It's a rather stupid response, but it serves a worthy purpose.

On the walk home I pose a riddle for Molly: "How do you make peace with an Italian mama?"

Through a bambina, of course.

# August 2  *Arms And The Girl*

Molly has discovered her hands and arms, simultaneously. Trouble is, poor thing, she can't control them both at the same time, so that when she reaches for something, she can't close her hand on it. When she closes her hand into a fist, she sacrifices the power of extension. The end effect is hands whirl and swipe to no purpose. I look forward to, as much as I fear, her putting the two together, melding reach and grasp, when nothing will escape her exploration. That should come soon.

She's also beginning to work her walker—the Tot Wheels II model that naturally works better on the slick tile floors, less well against the carpet's inertial drag. True, I've lowered the device to its lowest station and she has to practically stand on tiptoes to reach the floor, and her slender legs tire easily in it, but she's coming on. Really coming on. Like John Henry in the stretch. News flash for Tim when she gets home: Molly made clicking sounds with her tongue today.

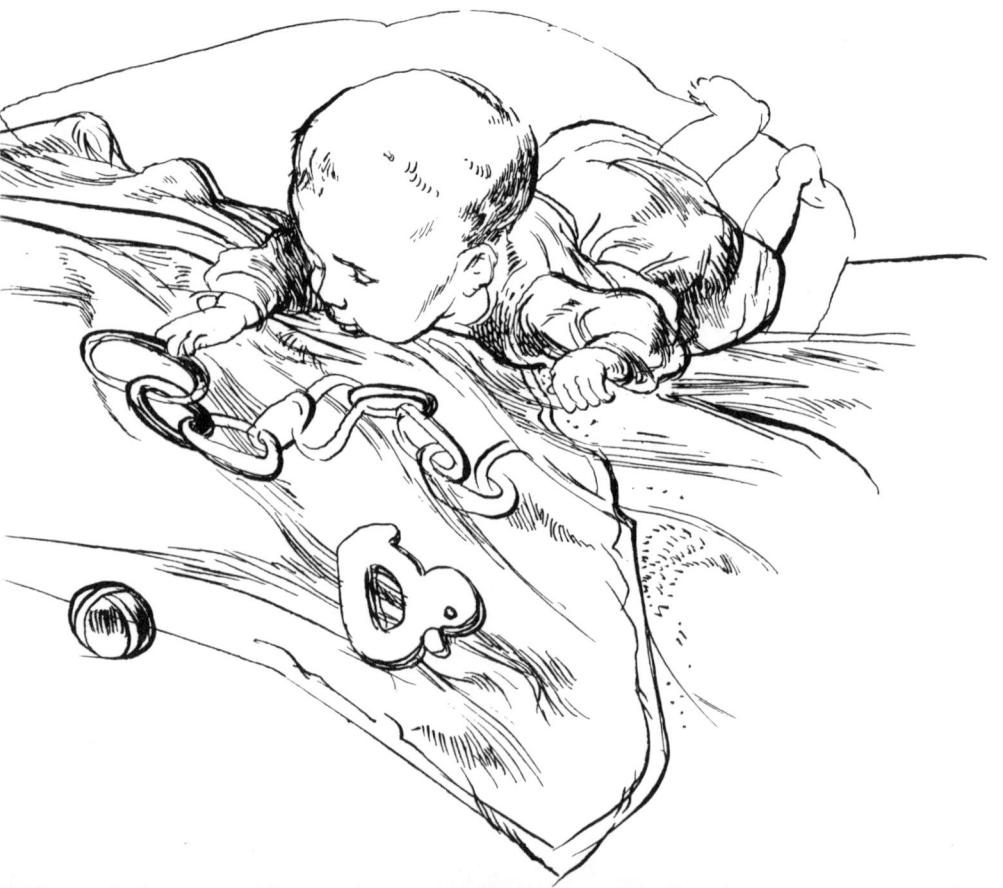

# August 3  *On The Move*

More progress in the walker. Molly's with me now in the writing room as I plug this into my Kaypro. The linoleum floor allows her to go on sudden scoots across the room, not where she's had any intention of going to be sure, but it is movement, and she likes that, and what she likes I like, as long as it gives me a little more writing time. Now and then I glance over at her to check. The bubbles go in, the bubbles come out...and then it's an upchuck.

As I wipe the creamy liquid off her mouth and chin and shirtfront, I marvel again at how she can go through the most violent regurgitations and still show no sign of pain or concern. I also marvel at her eyes, which have settled on a fetching steel blue.

In a little more than a hour's time the big oval eyes have drooped to half mast and she gets cross in earnest. Timarie comes in to my rescue on this lovely productive Sunday and "tops her off." She takes her in her arms and nurses Molly until her eyes close, and then I am summoned to do another finesse job.

Mercifully, Molly sleeps longer now—up to five uninterrupted hours at night, up to three during the day. And she sleeps soundly when she's not ailing. Ailing...aye, there's the rub. How many baby days are free of some minor ailment's pain or discomfort? Not many when you add them up. Yet, despite the flatulence that periodically sends her squirming and wailing for release and relief, Molly is no great trouble.

Certainly hers is a far scream from her brother Kurt's infancy, which was marked by three months of evening colic and must have got me several hundred years of sin remission in purgatory. Parents of colicky babies know how those guilt-giving, unrelievable cries of agony stretch one's patience and fray a marriage. Also, keep in mind that my son Kurt had a twin brother Karl, and a brother Eric only 15 months his senior, and they often voiced their dissatisfaction with life as it is, too. Sometimes as a chorus.

But what can you do except count your blessings, be them ever so few? First among them is that the mind forgets...and forgets pain first of all. Last is being around energetic new life and its young protoplasm, the keep of optimism, that you hope—and sometimes believe—rubs off.

# August 4        *Doubts And Resolutions*

I awake this morning with Molly to my right, noisily nursing with her back to me. For some reason, today it's a repulsive sight. She looks and sounds coarse, like a little piglet gorging itself.

Could I be wrong about her? My mind wanders guiltily to the curiosity I always feel in nurseries and the unseemly game I find myself playing. Scanning the bassinets for a rough total, I compute the percentage that stats say will be future felons (is there a murderer among them?) and try to isolate them; on to identifying the numerous drones doomed to live lives of quiet desperation. Then I try to pick out the achievers—those few who may advance the human cause by an inch or an ounce. Are there signs, hints, in their cries, the way they squirm in their swaddling?

Sick. Maybe. Maybe I ought to go and see a psychiatrist. No, I can't. In a mutation of that "never-sleep-with-someone-who-has-more-problems-than-you" maxim, I have never met a shrink with fewer problems than I, so that relief is not open to me.

Molly interrupts my writer's thoughts by rolling over to face me with a pink smile. How could I have doubted her?

At 9:13 a.m. I do what I've feared doing since I first set my mind to spending this summer with Molly. As I'm changing her diaper, she suddenly cuts loose with a scream that in tone and timbre I've never heard before. One of pure pain. I have physically hurt her.

I catch her up and pull her to my chest and coo my apologies, truly frightened, wondering whether I should call the fire department conveniently located just a half block away. Call a doctor? Tell Timarie? Or just cover it up and hope?

How could I have done such a thing? Over 20 minutes of nervous pacing and comforting, which slowly abate her cries, I reconstruct what must have happened. I was listening to a National Public Radio newscast on President Reagan's reluctance to impose economic sanctions on South Africa. My temper flared at the moral absurdity of sponsoring an illegitimate insurrection in Nicaragua while tolerating Pinochet's classic fascist dictatorship in Chile and accommodating a bunch of Afrikaner arch-bigots. My anger expressed itself in a rough punch to Molly's abdomen as I was fastening the final safety pin.

Have I learned nothing in 53 years? Rage at the external world's stupidities accomplishes nothing, except to consume the self. Condemn folly, yes, but save the energy for the small picture—family and friends, and especially one's children, whom you can hope to influence. That's where to right wrongs. Teach Molly to love and respect others—and do it all better than I'm able to do. That's how I do my part.

World events too often become public distractions from what is privately important. Love, or its lack, within a family. Charity, or our indifference, toward those we meet this very day.

This good feeling gets a little reinforcement at the butcher shop, where I've toted Molly in our Napsak. As I wait at the counter for my half a salmon to be wrapped, a middle-aged woman stops in front of us as though to frame a picture. "That's pretty," she says. "That's perfect."

# August 5     *The Heroines Among Us*

We've got many errands to run today, so I put Molly in our Napsak as soon as she's gulped down her morning six ounces. Great to be alive. Another bright and sunny California day that Molly is missing because she's fallen asleep.

I've worked up a sweat by the time I reach the Bank of America branch, where I wait in line to make a small deposit. At the teller's window I notice a flashing message board behind the counter. "Ask us about auto loans" it advises. Good idea. Just this morning I've mailed off an application for an auto loan to the teachers' credit union, without bothering to do any rate shopping. "What's your rate on auto loans?"

The young woman tells me politely that she can't help me, but points across the room. "See someone on the platform."

Platform? I look down and see that the bank is divided down the middle, the tellers' half in marble and the other, which is indeed slightly raised, in carpet, where there are fewer folks and they're better dressed.

"I'd like to get a quote on auto loans," I inform the first young woman I come to.

She seems flustered, mutters something to me, and gets up from her desk and walks, in those quiet mincing steps bank employees take, toward the front of the building. I guess I'm supposed to follow her and I do. But when I get up there I find four chairs, two of them occupied by waiting customers.

Hey! I'm not going to sit down. That might wake Molly. Besides, I don't have a lot of time to waste for just a quote.

By then young woman number one has alerted more-mature woman number two, who briskly approaches me and says, with the hushed voice one reserves for visits to Saint Peter's or Westminster Abbey, "you'll have to see the manager."

"Fine! Great!" I start following her back toward the center of the bank.

But mature woman is quicker than I and hurries up to a dignified man in shirt and tie and whispers something. The dignified man, whom I now can identify as the manager from the placard on his desk, rises from that desk and walks past me. "Please take a seat," he whispers, gesturing toward the chair facing his desk.

"I can't. It'll wake the baby," I protest. But I don't think he's heard because he's gone over to the tellers' side, where he's fidgeting with something.

What the hell is going on? And then comes the dawn. I'm an embarrassment—a bloody eyesore! A big shambling geek dressed in a bright red sweatsuit, and probably smelling pretty ripe, too, standing right in the center of their crowded bank with a papoose hanging from his neck!

Strangely, I'm delighted with the discovery. I nix my decision to leave in the interest of time and choose to wait it out instead.

The bank manager sees this and approaches me a second time. "Please, sit down," he says as he passes me and heads toward his desk. As I follow him I again explain why I can't accept his kind offer. When I reach his desk he beckons me to take a chair yet again.

"I can't."

He seems not able to believe his ears.

"I might wake my baby." Thrust home! I have switched from the innocuous definite article to the cloying possessive adjective. My baby. Gagghh! For a split second he looks at me as though I might be a fugitive from the Fairview Mental Hospital. Then suddenly he's all poise and professionalism.

Standing at my side, without ever even acknowledging that I am carrying a baby, which I continue patting gently on the back throughout, he pencils out the computations of my 60-month loan. It comes to 11 percent.

I thank him for his trouble. But I can get 10.9 from the credit union.

He doesn't seem to regret losing the business.

I walk triumphantly on to the supermarket where I pick up about eight pounds of food. (I've discovered that ten pounds, along with Molly's ten-plus, is about all I can tote home from this distance.) The cashier at the checkout stand hasn't seen Molly for a month and asks if I'd unzip her bag so she can see her. I do and Molly's little red head pops out, her eyes wide open.

"How she's grown!," the cashier exclaims.

"She's so sweet. How cute," chant a mother and young daughter in unison on my left.

At that moment Molly vomits on Ralphs' counter.

But I am not nonplused. I am in command. Out of the Napsak's left front pocket comes a diaper and the white spot vanishes as though it had never sullied the conveyor belt.

"You really come prepared," says the mother with admiration.

"Yep, we come prepared for anything."

Our walk home is attended by a half-dozen smiling mothers' faces, the last one of them the most memorable. She is a thin, sandy-haired woman who appears to be in her late twenties; she approaches wearing the same type of Napsak I do, with two toddlers in tow. She looks haggard, used up. Until she smiles and I see into her eyes. She is radiant.

I have come to love these women with small children and babies, and those furtively curious women about to have babies. Forget the statesmen and movie queens and football stars and barons and baronesses of industry. Barring the great artist and the breakthrough scientist—the Beethovens and Einsteins, the Joyces and Plancks and Picassos, that precious few—most of us are really quite expendable and replaceable. Despite our vigorous protests to the contrary, we have not that much to offer, don't make that much of a difference. But those who carry life and nurture it do. To me they now seem the best and enduring expressions of our civilization. They are the embodiment of love, the glue of family and civilized society, and I'm ashamed it took me so long to appreciate it.

Shame is personal. But concern becomes general...at least for this closet moralist. Americans pay lip service to the family's core place in the life and health of our republic. We like to say our children are our future.

You'd never know it from the bottom rung child care occupies on the status ladder. You'd never know it from a government that through actions and inaction consistently undervalues the timeless arts of mothering and fathering.

Warring on drugs is fine. Rooting out corruption and deceit in government and the marketplace is essential. Defending our principles of democracy and individual freedom at home and abroad is laudable. But isn't it time for a reshuffling of priorities, where the pressures on working parents and their young get attention and relief? An organism's health radiates from its nuclei.

# August 6     *Games People Play*

The ear picks up the slightly altered hunger cry that communicates more...distress, as when Molly's arm or leg is snared between cradle slats. I rush to her, free her this early a.m.

She always opens happy eyes, grants the quick open smile on her sleep-rouged face. I love to lift her up and stretch her out on my chest and have her cling to me as she completes her waking up.

I just wish she hadn't learned to make fists in my chest hairs. So slight a girl, and yet so strong in what she can physically do.

Nowadays she lifts her head and trunk on extended arms to look around. And she will not be denied. Another of her gathering strengths is stiffening her whole body—usually in resistance to something Mom and Dad want her to do—with the muscle-steel of a gymnast. This skill, I would observe, is better applied when she stiffens just her legs—an inchoate expression of the determination to walk, to get around on her own, thank you! Take her hands and pull her to you and she's standing, as if she wanted to be upright all along....Unless she can be high up on Dad's shoulder, a vantage she loves for ogling all things new, surveying the big picture from above. Yes, she prefers looking down on her world.

Timarie refines this gain into a game tonight and calls it "Water Ski." Tim tucks her thumbs into Molly's hands-become-fists. "OK, hit it," she shouts, pulling her hands back. Molly's legs stiffen and up she rises, riding the rug or a belly or a bedspread with a conquering grin.

I'm mildly jealous. I should have thought of this game. I'm her mummer-mimer-fool—her poppa. That's my department.

# August 7     *Not Done Yet*

Once again Molly opens the morning with a smile, which I provoke with my mugging as I lift her from her crib. I delight in her sudden expressions of delight at my many facial contortions, which I work mostly when we are alone. All kids love clowns.

Whatever the source of Molly's fine grimace (and forget about my crabbed age, and ignore all those who are not daily near an infant or do not remember what a joy of reawakening wonder that nearness brings), those who have young children know the powerful tonic of a child's smile.

Molly and I have hit our best stride. At the market today she thrashes around the Napsak until I unzip it to where she can check out the merchandise. She's especially taken with the fruits and vegetables; she gawks at them, gurgles her pleasure. She dozes at the bank, peers out at the line of patrons at the post office, falls asleep at the cleaners. We do four miles in all.

After dinner Timarie remarks that I look like I've lost a little weight.

Arthritis, thou shalt die!

# August 8     *What I've Learned*

After a shrimp-stew dinner with Rod and Heidi, rinsed down with a fine domestic sauvignon blanc (Rod is going to be the next master chef of New Orleans, not I), they spread the map of California out on the floor. They are driving north with little Aaron in their Westfalia and plan to spend a month camping in the northern part of the state, which they've scarcely seen. They want me, a one-time travel writer and long-time editor of Californiana, to recommend what to see.

As I make suggestions, they trigger memories of my old roving days...years really...many years. I get excited and the itch to go myself. Suddenly, I realize I'm envious...but it passes.

This summer, my place is in the home, with Molly. Not only do I have an experiment to conclude, for my own satisfaction if no one else's, but I'm actually enjoying my househusband role—most of the time, anyway. And I'm learning. About myself. And, in a very unscientific but useful way, what babies are all about.

The major revelation? That "bonding," as the human behaviorists like to call the deep emotional attachment between two humans, takes place largely through ordinary contact. It seems to me that, except for that one imponderable, the breast-feeding connection, where some deeper tie is probably nourished, the sex of the most-present parent—the one baby looks for and smiles at—is not a factor. Timarie agrees.

Anything else? I think so. Just a conclusion empirically drawn, from much too small a sample, yes, but I believe there are behavioral differences between boy and girl babies, even before those hormones start flowing. When I held my boys, they would give me maybe a minute, then whine and squirm until they got free of my grasp.

Not so my Molly on the second go-around. She snuggles and clings closely to me for just as long as I'll let her, all love and surrender.

Finally, that it is easier to be a parent the second time around. You've been over the course before and remember a few of the dips and turns. You don't panic as readily or worry so much, and your patience with piercing cries and frantic, non-stop movement has stretched farther then you thought possible. Permeating all is the older father's constant knowing that the time he'll be with his child on earth is cruelly short, and that he should hug the feeling out of every moment.

# August 9   *Tactile Pleasures*

"Nor can foot feel, being shod...."
The line from Hopkins' "God's Grandeur" streaks into my mind as I watch Timarie introduce Molly to the feel of grass on bare feet in our backyard. Molly in the walker tentatively, inquiringly pokes her little toes out at the bending blades. She stares at this new and wonderful carpet. She likes it. Ah! The simple pleasures!

On this sunny summer Saturday Timarie decides Molly should also be introduced to what being a California Girl is all about. Time for her beach debut, while Dad stays home to catch up on his journal.

The report back is that Molly absolutely loved it...especially the feel of sand on her toes. Clearly, daughter has inherited mother's sybaritic tendencies.

After Timarie and I finish dinner, I decide to peek in on Molly to see if she's asleep yet, and whether she's kicked her covers off. I carefully turn the doorknob as I push the door down and away from me, because otherwise it sticks and makes a loud scraping noise sure to wake her. Successfully done! I sneak in and stand off to the side of her cradle. The little imp! She's spied me out of the corner of her eye and starts crying. She wants up and out where the action is. She has also inherited Mom's night-owl tendencies.

# August 10    *Derby Results And First Tears*

I still can't believe it! In the *Times* this morning I read that the young mother whose twins died in July is being charged with involuntary manslaughter and involuntary child endangerment, which, upon conviction, can result in sentences of two, four, or six years in prison! The police say that the young divorcee left the little boy and girl in the locked car for about an hour. The woman, who has already spent five nights in County Jail, is quoted as saying, "It seems like they'd realize there isn't much worse punishment than the hurt I feel now." Amen!

"Come quick and bring the camera," Timarie yells. "Molly is crying her first tears."

I bolt from my morning stint at the keyboard and scramble to find the Canon, which is seldom where I remember leaving it.

I arrive and Molly clams up. She stares up at me.

"See the tear?" Timarie asks, dabbing with a diaper under Molly's right eye.

I can't admit that I don't. "I guess so."

"What took you so long...you didn't get the shot."

"I was reading. Come on, Molly, please cry," I plead to no avail. A second later the humor of my words hits me. I beg her for an hour to shut up, and then I suddenly want her to cry! What's a baby to do?

Getting Molly into the stroller for what's become a Sunday threesome's walk is a thankless chore. She's still too small to fit the contrivance, and on this stripped-down, bottom-of-the-line Strolee bought for a bargain $20 on a close-out there are no fancy do-dads that allow you to adjust for fit. Yet we go through the motions, trying to prop her up when her head snaps forward onto the tray, or lists too far right or left, as we bump along over the uneven sidewalk pavement panels.

This evening Timarie declares the results of the Diaper Derby official. In a slow time (translating from track parlance as intermittent and so-so results), it's... well, kind of a three-way dead heat for first. A&D is best for burns. Lotrisone is best for yeast. And plain old Vaseline is best for protecting the bum once it's all cleaned up. Desitin, Ammens and Polysporin also ran.

## August 11        *A Brother's Gift*

From the start, one of my cares—not really a worry—in becoming a second-generation father was that the two sets of offspring like one another. (Love one another may be too much to ask, even of full-blooded siblings.) A gap of 19 years may help or hinder; I'm yet to find that out. But I do know that less-than-friendly divorces can set up certain snags in the hoped-for harmony in advance. You try your best to tie them down as they show themselves.

From the start I referred to the coming child as "your sister" when talking to my sons. Technically, we all know that she's a half-sister, but I don't think many of us are really such sticklers for biological fact that we would say, "Why don't you walk your half-sister to the store?"

So far, I have been very lucky. Eric and Karl, who live away, are friendly and curious about Molly during those brief, infrequent times they are here. Resident Kurt has from the first shown a hearty liking for Molly, talking to her and drawing out smiles. But ultimately 19-year-old boys are interested in 18-year-old girls not related to them by blood, and not in a baby sister or half-sister.

You can imagine my happy surprise to find tonight—the eve of our first wedding anniversary—a gift wrapped and marked for Molly in Kurt's hand. Inside are two toys that don't comfortably fit in the budget of a part-time boxboy: a "Flutterball"—two painted plastic butterflies affixed to a spinning plastic rod that extends the full hollow diameter of the clear plastic sphere, thus allowing the butterflies to seemingly fly as the ball is moved or rolled; the second is Fisher-Price's "Three Men in a Tub," four-inch-high figures of the Butcher, Baker and Candlestickmaker with a bright yellow tub (with interior bell) to stand in, all made in the manufacturer's traditional, sturdy, child-safe mode.

No surprise that the two gifts have become her favorites, supplanting a ring of plastic keys and a plastic chain of many-colored "boomerings" with snap-together links. The Flutterball immediately gets a good licking over (never mind the butterflies inside). And the yellow-clad Butcher and the white-clad Baker (not so much the red-clad Candlestickmaker) are clutched and pressed tight against her drool-drenched shirtfront.

Should the novelty of her previous toys wear off that fast? Or is Molly just an impatient, easily bored redheaded little girl?

# August 12     *How The Cookie Crumbles*

This is our one-year anniversary, and we had big plans to sit down with the videotapes of our wedding and the snapshots and the slides of that momentous day in Sligo a year back and relive it with Molly, front row and center. Not to be. Timarie has a heavy workday and I have two meetings with new faculty and a returning student in need of advising at school. We'll postpone the show till Saturday. Instead, we'll go out to dinner at the Japanese restaurant where Timarie first proposed marriage to me, and I accepted. (Honesty forces me to add that it followed by a year my proposal to her, which hadn't earned a definite "yes" or "no.") Molly will stay with Timarie's mother, the first time she's been baby-sat in the evening.

My meetings go well—particularly the last one, with Tom, the student, during which a delivery man arrives with two dozen white carnations (my favorites because they were my mother's favorites) surrounding a lone pink rose, representing Molly. "Sparky: Thank you for my best year. I love you. Springtime," reads the card.

Tom reads my face and more. "This baby-sitting must really agree with you."

"Why do you say that?"

"You're looking good....You were really looking beat in May."

I prefer to think he's not buttering me up for future grades. He's an A−/B+ student now, so he doesn't need the grade points.

"You really think so?"

"Yeah....You're looking younger."

Ha! Have I stumbled upon the secret of reversing aging? Years ago I read that the best method yet found, by wise men in the Near East, was to breathe the breath of a young woman. I've been doing that faithfully. Have I now discovered my own corollary: stay home and mind baby?

I tell Timarie about my rejuvenation over our sushi and tempura, washed down with just enough Kirin, before we get into reminiscing. It was June 2, 1984 and she took me to dinner here at Koi in Seal Beach, behaved very nervously for reasons I hadn't guessed, until the waitress arrived with the check and a plate of fortune cookies.

Fortune cookies? In a Japanese restaurant? I had spent two-plus years in Japan during the Korean War and I never saw a fortune cookie. Mentally, I wrote it all off as one more domestic cultural corruption so common in our melting pot. Then I broke it open for my fortune: "Lare, will you marry me?"

Of course I said yes.

I meant to build on that precedent this evening. Unfortunately, as usual in such delicate matters, I've botched it. Forgotten my own jimmied cookie in the car.

Once, the nervous new mom gets up from dinner to call her mom to see how Molly's doing. This time gap, though, is not long enough for me to slip out to the car and fetch the cookie before she returns to the table. That would really blow it—get caught in the act, stealing back to your seat with an altered fortune clutched in your hand. Not now.

As we get into the car I reach into the back seat. "You missed dessert, didn't you?" I ask as I hand her the cookie in the dark. Timarie laughs in relief. "I thought you forgot to get me anything," she says as she opens the cookie and turns on the toplight to read its message: "I'm glad you asked. I'm glad I said yes."

# August 13    *Seven Come Eleven*

I love symmetry, analogues, a priori "truths." They feed my hope that there is purpose in the universe.

Today at three-month-old Molly's doctor's visit (yes, three, that mystical magical number again) Molly weighs 11 pounds, 7 ounces, just the reverse of her birthweight of 7 pounds, 11 ounces. I hope that portends cosmic order, and not merely a future in Las Vegas. She also lengthens out at an even 24 inches in height, which is divisible by three even while maintaining its English distance-measuring system's integrity.

Should I brag about how confident and competent I was on my first solo to the pediatrician's office? How I went about my business talking to my girl as I undressed her and weighed her and changed her and then dressed her again, deftly plugging a bottle of half-and-half in her mouth when she started complaining? Did I impress the nurse and nurses' aide with my successful invasion of "woman's domain?" Did I exhibit my parental competence in front of Dr. Chang?

The answer to all the above is "yes."

"I forgot to ask Dr. Chang today, but don't you think we should start thickening Molly's daytime bottles?"

"What?" Timarie challenges, rather acerbically.

"You know. . . put some rice cereal or the like in her milk—something that will stick to her ribs."

"Didn't you hear me discuss that with Dr. Chang weeks ago? Babies don't need or digest cereals at this age. We start when she's six months old."

Am I a perfect mother? The answer is no.

# August 14     *Her First Statement*

I lift a whining Molly from her walker to my lap, as I start the morning plunking at the Kaypro. It works. Her tiny fingers leap to the keys; "ddz vrdf xxxxzz" is her maiden literary statement as a chip-age scribe. No wonder she was complaining; she just wanted to do what she's seen Dad doing.

Molly is also trying to talk. At least I think the narrow range of noises she makes are meant to communicate with us.

"Is that Swahili or Urdu you're speaking?" I ask as I try to guide her mid-morning bottle into her mouth. Her tinny, two-syllable response sounds to me like "er-doo."

"I thought so."

Molly should be a verbal child, given the parents she has. Timarie, taking her cue from Heidi, certainly pushes it. She reads to Molly aloud as they are nursing, which makes for some odd middle-of-the-night awakenings for me, dropped right into the middle of some profound discussion of Nietzsche or deep-from-the-heart confessions of seasoned lovers.

So far Timarie has read Molly Kundera's *The Unbearable Lightness of Being* and they are now well into *The Dubliners*. What a start!

"Molly's going to be one of the great women of history," I impulsively blurt out to Timarie, who's just finished feeding Molly and is now burping her.

Molly spits up a goodly stream of breakfast.

"What about her digestive habits?" Timarie taunts.

"Maybe we could hire a live-in maid whose only duty would be to follow her around and wipe up her barf."

Molly jams a whole fist into her mouth and starts gumming it; the hand glistens with drool.

Rome was not built in a day.

And queens are made, not born.

# August 15     *Love On A Pendulum*

Timarie is asleep. Molly is awake at her side, making all manner of facial expressions and attempting to reach out and touch her mother. No dice, so she reaches down and discovers her toes, which occupy her fingers for ten magical moments—until Mom wakes up and the breast is bared. At which sight all distractions end and the serious business of eating begins, with Molly-the-voluptuary intent on sucking, while abstractedly and rhythmically flexing her fingers and toes.

At breakfast's end, while Timarie is still burping her, Molly turns her head and gives me a smile that rates a 9 on the Chernobyl Scale.

"You get the smile, you change her."

"OK." I accept the challenge, before I find there's been an explosion at the mustard factory.

I then go on to coax nine successive smiles from Molly's joyful face, and probably would have continued on to set a new world's record for the Guinness book had not the jealous mother poked her head between us.

"I feel left out around here."

"I get smiles, but I don't get any peace and quiet," I say to appease.

Ten minutes later Molly starts crying in my arms. Why? "Is she hungry? Tired?"

"No, she just probably wants her mother," Timarie says in the on-going tug-of-war.

She's right. Another pendulum swing.

Early this evening, as my chicken-sausage-and-navy-bean casserole cooks, I notice that I have poured my beer into a tupperware "glass" and it's resting on a breast shield in lieu of a coaster. Sure signs all of my late domestic state, no doubt.

# August 16     *An Irish Wedding Revisited*

**M**olly sleeps this morning as her parents, per their promise, travel down memory lane from their just-delivered leather sofa. Tim and I have memory-goaders galore, including our album of wedding photos, two separate videotapes of the marriage ceremony, and some random 35-millimeter slides one or the other of us somehow managed to squeeze off that strange and signal day exactly one year and four days ago.

    It had been my idea first to get married away from family, friends, acquaintances. Yes, I wanted to deny them all the spectacle of this April-October match, escape with my blushing bride in pink the hassle of arrangements, the hectorings of Tim on preparations, the reception gossip and the multitudinous mutterings of "it'll-never-last" kibbitzers. Wouldn't it be great to go abroad, say, for a runaway romantic escapade? Among total strangers? Tim agreed. "I want to enjoy *myself*," she said. "I don't want to have to worry about whether other people are enjoying *themselves*."

    And so the caper was jointly planned, suddenly and in rare total agreement, and to this day neither of us can remember what idea got first voice by whom. The wedding would be performed in Ireland, which Larry, though ten years a travel writer and three years an airman abroad, had somehow missed in his peregrinations; specifically, the wedding would be in Sligo, where Larry had long wanted to go on literary pilgrimage during the yearly International Yeats Summer School in August. Father Dave, a priest Timarie had kept in contact with, and who left his Pico Rivera, California, church most summers to visit his family in Ireland, would perform the ceremony—with an otherwise pick-up cast—in Sligo. To get there we'd fly to Shannon a week before the planned wedding day, rent a car and drive up through Yeats country around Gort, to Galway, chase the sun to Connemara, and then weave northeast back to Sligo, arriving a comfortable two and a half days before the Monday morning marriage. After the vows, we would drive back to Shannon, fly to Paris (which Timarie had not yet seen) for a honeymoon week, then on to London for another week (which came to include a few days' try at parenthood), then fly back to Southern California. And the division of labor? All the travel arrangements were Larry's to make. Timarie would take care of the rest.

It is my deep belief—admittedly based on limited personal experience—that weddings for men at best are things got through without much memory of them. I hope I don't anger feminists by saying I believe that, again based on a small sample, most women hold them in higher regard. No, I'll go farther. That many women consider wedding days among the three most important days in their lives. That a few even make at-home or runaway productions of them worthy a Cecil B. DeMille.

Tim ranks between the many and the few—leaning to the runaway few. I'd swear if she wasn't Irish that she was Helmuth Von Moltke's great-great-great grandaughter, so incredibly efficient was she in matters of organization and logistics. Among the things she arranged, long distance, by letter:

Confirming church availability for the appointed day, and the north-from-Cork travel plans of Father Dave.

Hiring a Sligo photographer, Donncha, to photograph the wedding.

Hiring a videotaper, Peter, to record the event in image and sound for posterity.

Closer to home, she designed and had made the wedding rings and her wedding dress (an ecru silk drop-waist with lace overskirt and peach hip sash), located in Beverly Hills after much searching a haberdasher who would attach a veil to the cream wool hat she had bought months before, assisted me in the choice of a tailor-made dark-blue wool-and-silk suit of trim Italian cut that threatened to stave in my middle-aged hips, found and bought for me a long long-sleeved shirt that matched her dress and a peach-colored Irish linen tie that matched her wedding dress's sash.

On departure day Tim carefully packed the dress and suit into a carry-on hanging bag, the hat into a carry-on hatbox, and the rest of our gear—including a boxed bottle of Dom Perignon given to us by her brother John to be drunk on our wedding night to launch the marriage—into the suitcases. I carried them to the check-in counter. Destination: the Emerald Isle.

Despite the first-day breakdown of our Toyota Starlet rent-a-car, a half-day wait in a thick Irish mist for its replacement, and the all-but-constant gray skies and intermittent downpours, the six-day pre-nuptial journey was a high-spirited meander north, with Timarie learning and mastering early the wrong-side-of-the-road driving on slick and narrow country lanes lined with stone walls, while I sat jack-kneed and terrified (she compensated for the encroaching stone walls at what I thought was a critical margin between us and the oncoming traffic) beside her, the official navigator and map reader. Nightly we rested and gathered courage at friendly bed-and-breakfasts.

Thursday we thought we'd more than solved the matron-of-honor problem when we met in the castle at Kinvara traveling twin sisters from the States, Sharon and Sheila; though they had family business in County Mayo, they would rendezvous with us for the Sligo wedding, and left two phone numbers where they could be reached.

More reassuringly, Father Dave—despite on-again, off-again car trouble on his drive up from Cork—joined us early Sunday afternoon, just in time for the three of us to take in the opening lecture of the Yeats festival. Afterwards we dined together on Atlantic salmon at the Ballincar House hotel, where in May I had reserved, by phone and letter, rooms for us. Then we drove toward the late, high-latitude sunset at the end of Rosses' Point, where Yeats the boy listened to sailors' tales of smugglers hard by his "gong-tormented" sea. Together we walked the pebbly strand. Father Dave gathered up a handful of seashells. "Give these to your grandchildren," he said, dropping them in Timarie's cupped palms. (I would see them again ten months later, in Molly's room, piled in a small crystal cup given to her by her grandmother, high up on a knick-knack shelf.)

We found a pub and over pints of Harp lager spoke of important things...eternity, infinity, apparent celestial harmonies, and the rather sorry state of things on earth...not excluding calamity-ridden Ireland. As a reluctant Irish twilight eased into dark, we headed back to the Ballincar for a nightcap.

I should say that some hitches also developed on our action-packed pre-wedding day. Though the photographer and videotaper were contacted and instructed, Timarie couldn't arrange for the bridal flowers she had her heart set on. "Nothing's open on an Ireland Sunday except the churches and the bars," she complained. More aggravating, she had trouble connecting with her honored matrons; she left instructions at both County Mayo numbers, but one respondent seemed dismayed by the message and the other spoke only an English subverted by Gaelic.

I wish I could say I handled it all with worldly wise assurance, as befitted my age and experience. Sorry. Rather, I felt like a decrepit rogue and peasant slave, vaguely guilty of Socrates' crime but without his wisdom, intimidated as always by ceremony and the demands it put on me—a man who since earliest boyhood had felt himself a hypersensitive male outsider whose only protection was to become a sentimentiphobic outsider. Following our agreed-upon nightcap in the Ballincar's bar, I resorted on this memorable night to my best defense against the emotional creepy-crawlies: I excused myself with "goodnights," walked alone upstairs, and stretched out on the bed. Sleep gobbled me up within seconds.

Timarie, meanwhile, stayed below for a last try at reaching her promised matrons, impressing into service the weary desk clerk, who by birth or experience or both had to be wiser to a telephone system I would euphemistically call "quaint." Alas! The frazzled Irish lady had no better luck than my wife-soon-to-be; the latter, resourceful to a fault, seized the opportunity to make sure an ironing board would be delivered to our room for Monday-morning pressing of the wedding garments, and ice would come to chill the postnuptual champagne; then she pulled off the coup of coups.

At 37 minutes past midnight the phone rang.
"Hello?"
"Sparky, come on down."
"Tim?"
"Who else would be calling your room?"
"Where are you?"
"Downstairs. In the bar."
"In the bar?"
"Hurry! I got us a matron of honor and a best man! They want to meet you. I've also got us a flower girl and a ring bearer."
"Are you sober?"
"No. But come on down. You'll love them."

I call it the "Irish Phenomenon." Drift into any pub, order a pint, look right or left into a friendly face and the lilting words start flowing like crystal water from a spring mountain stream. Ale and stout and lager abet these upwellings of goodwill, the soaring music of what in Ireland may be only ordinary speech. And in that speech you'll hear more thrown-away wit than in a lifetime of watching Johnny Carson.

Kieran and Evelyn Byrne proved the apotheosis of that phenomenon. In their middle thirties, he had a Ph.D in history and she taught Anglo-Irish literature in secondary schools, and with their eleven-year-old daughter Aoife and seven-year-old son Kieran Jr., (both of whom were upstairs in their hotel room asleep), they were motoring from Cork to Donegal on holiday, with two days set aside to pop in on lectures at the Yeats International Summer School; one of those days they were now—on this late-night lark!—willing to give up to a needy and unlikely pair of Yanks.

"What are you drinking?" Kieran asked as I took the fourth chair at their table and a middle-aged waitress approached.

"A glass of Harp." I told the waitress.

"A pint of Harp," he instructed the bartendress, pointing at me for what would not be the last time that early morning of Timarie's wedding day.

How can I describe the next two hours, except to say that the four of us discussed such manageable tidbits as God, religion, literature, justice, truth, honor, beauty, American and Irish politics, and discussed them intelligently, comprehensively. . .or so it seemed in the lovely haze of a Harp and Whiskey accompaniment. If only we had taped it.

One thing I do remember was Evelyn saying, deep into a discussion of Irish poetry, that if it "hadn't been for about ten poems" Yeats wrote late in life, "he would have been remembered as a very good Irish poet, but not the great poet the world reveres." She was right. I'd never thought of that. And I knew the ten poems.

At 2:25 a.m. the four of us agreed that to make the noon wedding, we would have to get some sleep. Reluctantly, we headed to our rooms.

"I'll knock at 10:30 to help you dress," Evelyn said to Timarie at the foot of the hotel's stairs.

"Good," said Tim. "I'll order flowers in the morning. I'll get a bouquet for Oeifa, too."

Evelyn looked almost suspiciously at us. "People just don't do this, you know," she said, for about the fourth time.

"I know," Tim agreed. "But we are."

At 9:29 a.m., dressed in my new blue suit, cream-colored shirt and peach-colored Irish-linen tie—all freshly pressed by the bride-to-be—I vacated the Ballincar's best guest room. It wasn't proper that I see the bride before she donned her wedding dress. Besides, I was out of Irish pounds, and there was a chance I'd be expected to spring for something during the day. It turned out Father Dave was flat, too. Why not run to the bank together? We'd take my car. But Father Dave would drive, because I didn't trust myself on the left side of the road, not when a light rain had slickened the pavement, and certainly not on my wedding day.

Our entrance into the Sligo Branch of the Bank of Ireland was not without ceremony. As we mounted the marble steps, a carryall full of Irish soldiers armed with submachine guns pulled to their chests brushed by us and to our flanks in full run. Hey! What was going on? I only came to exchange 80 dollars for pounds—a very minor transaction, really.

Once we'd changed our money, exited the bank through two walls of armed men at the ready and left them behind, Father Dave explained what was probably up. The Irish Republican Army had been on a bank-robbing spree lately to finance their war, and local police were not equipped to handle them. A tip probably put the army troops on alert.

Back at the Ballincar House Hotel our wait began. It has been my observation that all humans fall into one of two groups: those who are compulsively and nervously early for all events of pith, and those who are invariably late, whether it's a matter of moment or not. As I paced the hotel lobby in a semi-circle around the stairs the bride was to descend, I pondered the enduring enigma why those in the former camp always link up with those in the latter? And why they both then remain frustratingly stuck in their ways, making no converts?

At 11 a.m. by the lobby clock Father Dave, still worried about his car's will to carry on, departed for the church. Leaving me temporarily alone with my fears, awaiting my bride. Then Donncha arrived with his cameras to keep me company. Nervous company. We paced together. What could be keeping her?

(Unbeknownst to me, she was showering and washing her hair in an Irish shower typically short on water pressure. She dried the hair she had intentionally grown long for me for our wedding day. She was painstakingly ironing her silk satin dress on a veteran ironing board covered with two pillow cases from our bed because she feared the iron's steam would draw up onto the silk some of the venerable brown stains on the ironing board cover. She and Evelyn steamed the veil on her hat. She phone-ordered the flowers—two bouquets, one flower girl's basket, boutonnieres for the men and the traditional bouquet for the Virgin Mary. She phoned instructions to Donncha to be on hand for her stairway descent into the arms of her husband-to-be. She gave travel directions to Sharon—one of the twins who was tentatively promised in Kinvara a matron-of-honor role but who had on her own re-established contact by a morning phone call; Tim had to tell her that she'd been replaced by an authentic Irish matron of honor, but she nevertheless wanted to come, but couldn't bring her sister Sheila, who was under the weather, but would come with her brother Mike, who would videotape the event—a redundancy that honored one and all—or was it one and few?—participating in the ceremony.)

I paced faster. A case of the nerves. There was only one remedy—one I always resort to before IRS audits and airplane boardings. I went into the bar and ordered a morning pint—not an unheard of practice in the Emerald Isle. "Relax," I told myself. "It's probably the last time you'll have to go through one of these." I felt better already. So, not knowing whether the advice or the lager was working the magic, I ordered another pint...to break the tie, as it were. Conclusion? The advice was playing second fiddle to the Harp.

I was feeling downright well and wishing for a mouthful of Listerine when the late, great moment came. Timarie, shining in cream and peaches and looking younger than springtime, slowly descended the stairs to a small-but-applauding gathering of wedding party and hotel staff. Slowly because Donncha, the photographer and perfectionist, told Timarie to stop on every other gold-checked stairway carpet step for "one more."

Once Timarie came among us, I curled my left arm around her waist and she embraced me to genuine, but very brief, effusions. We were all late! For a very important date! Precisely how late I didn't know, because Timarie had made me shed my watch, as tradition bade.

The dutiful Donncha drove off in a hurry or a huff. Kieran and Evelyn, flower girl Aoife and ringbearer-designate Kieran, Jr, got into their little Toyota and waited for me to lead the way. But when I reached into my pants pocket for the ignition key I would turn over to Timarie, I came up with...nothing. Oh no! Father Dave had forgotten to give it back!

My panic at ever reaching the church on time got cut mercifully short. Bearded Peter, our amiable hired videotaper, drove up in a larger sedan. He had room for two more—three more, actually, if you forgot the yet-to-be-picked up flowers—and also happened to be going our way, which was southeast through Sligo Town to Achonry. To a wedding.

I followed Tim into the florist's, where she paid for the flowers—cream and pink carnations, the only blooms available. The young clerk's blue-green eyes shone with wonder and said it all: you don't order flowers the morning of your noon wedding—forget about picking them up *after* noon! Things are not done that way in Ireland. And that seemed reason enough for the young woman to take her own sweet time.

Timarie was frustrated. The more so when she discovered that Irish suits, like the one Kieran was wearing, had honest-to-god buttonholes for sticking in flower stems, while my Hong Kong special did not. So Tim asked the girl for a corsage pin. Didn't have one. Well then just a straight pin. Sorry. "Then do you have a *safety pin*!" A thin cutting edge in the voice. In a mere three minutes the clerk came up with a package of them, and Timarie stabbed through the white carnation and fixed it to her bridegroom's coat.

Things weren't done that way in Ireland....Well, maybe not just any day, but they would be this day, and heaven obviously approved, as would shortly be revealed. Tim passed out the bouquets and boutonnieres to the wedding party, put the Madonna's flowers in Peter's back window ledge, and the two-car caravan revved south. More than one road led to Achonry, it turned out, and Peter, mindful of the waiting priest and photographer and back-up videotaper and one ex-matron-of-honor-to-be, took a shortcut he knew. Fortunately, Father Dave knew it, and was divinely inspired to take it, too. Because that's where Peter spotted him, standing in the drizzle, eyes averted from the treacherous old Ford's raised hood, a thumb extended roadward, begging a lift.

The choice was quickly made that Peter's front seat be emptied of video gear (which could certainly be moved to my lap) and be offered to Father Dave, that Father Dave abandon his vehicle for the nonce, and that after the sacrament we'd find a garage.

All wedding ceremonies seem two hours too long to me. And hard to remember. Timarie tells me ours was beautiful, and she has two videotapes and 24 color stills to prove it. The only two things I clearly remember are that the sight of Timarie-as-a-young-bride Chernobyled me, and my reciting before Timarie, Father Dave, Kieran, Evelyn, their daughter and son, Sharon and Mike, Donncha and Peter of my interlinear, which wasn't really mine but borrowed, appropriately I thought, from Yeats, and appropriate to the occasion as well. It was his poem "He Wishes for the Cloths of Heaven," which goes:

> Had I the heavens' embroidered cloths,
> Enwrought with golden and silver light,
> The blue and the dim and the dark cloths
> Of night and light and the half-light,
> I would spread the cloths under your feet:
> But I, being poor, have only my dreams;
> I have spread my dreams under your feet;
> Tread softly because you tread on my dreams.

Exiting the church arm-in-arm with Tim was also memorable. Evelyn, bless her resourcefulness, had somehow found some confetti to shower us with while Donncha clicked away; and we walked into sudden sunlight, the shaft falling through a narrow blue break in the nimbal overcast, the first proof in six days that the sun passes over Ireland.

Neither Tim nor I had made any immediate post-nuptial plans, though I had hoped for a little time to chat more with Kieran and Evelyn, who had a mid-afternoon commitment to drive north to Donegal. First, though, there was the matter of Father Dave's car in need of repair. While the Brynes headed back to the Ballincar, Donncha drove home for lunch and Peter and the new bride and groom and the presiding padre drove around in the rain looking for a mechanic with a towing capability.

It is my impression that priests get preferential treatment in Ireland. I've had my share of breakdowns that entailed many hours of hassle in the allegedly more efficient United States; Father Dave, tended by several charitable souls, broke my service record by at least a half hour. He told us to go back to the hotel, electing to stay and watch the mechanic, the better to learn the contrary Ford's special whims and wants. He'd join us later and treat us to a wedding dinner.

The Byrnes were packed and ready to leave when we got back to the Ballincar. I pleaded with them in the lobby to stay, favor us in the bar with a last shared Harp. Just one. OK. And could the maitresse d' bring us something to eat . . . for what was sort of a reception? Yes, she could, from the little that was then available, and she did. . . .vegetable soup and some cold chicken on white bread and butter. I played taster and tried a chicken sandwich wedge. "A culinary masterpiece," I proclaimed. It was the first taste of food I'd had all day. And not a moment too soon.

Little Aoife, guarding her bouquet and using vocabulary we weren't used to hearing from an 11-year-old, said, "When the flowers have wilted, I'll replace them with fresh ones." She shyly asked Timarie and me to sign her autograph book. I wrote, "Best wishes to the prettiest little Irish girl I've ever met." She beamed. Then it was the sad time to go. Timarie and I and Peter with video camera in tow followed the Byrne family out to the hotel front parking lot.

Once again the mischievous little people who look after cars in Ireland intervened with comic relief. When the Byrnes ceased to wave goodbye and tried to enter their car, they couldn't. Little Kieran had locked the keys inside. Big Kieran said something I couldn't make out. I think it was

Gaelic for "being very upset."

"Do you have a coat hanger?" Peter asked them. It turned out that the matron of honor and best man did have a coat hanger—several of them—but they were inside the auto, doing their primary job. Again to the rescue came Peter the Indispensable. He happened to have one, in his car, which was unlocked. Yes, but why?

Peter pointed out that there was a third of an inch of open space on the driver's side, and that by rebending the hangar's metal one could fashion a handy entry tool. So deftly did he fashion this tool and put it to effective use that a few suggestions were made that he was a reformed car thief. Peter took the ribbing good-naturedly, stopping from time to time to step back and videotape his progress and his respectful audience. Too soon the car was opened, the travelers repeated their farewells, the laughter faded, and the friends scarcely made were a diminishing speck under Ben Bulben.

Peter, too, had to get going. Another goodbye to a brand new friend we might not see again. The time was 4:14 p.m. by my retrieved watch. For the first time on that frenetic day, I felt my spirits flag. As we walked back into the lobby lounge, sat down alone at our table and quietly picked at the last of the chicken sandwiches, I sensed a letdown in Timarie, too. It was too early to be suddenly alone.

Once more heaven came to our aid through a trio of Yeats festival attenders who burst into the lounge in a brisk, tripartite conversation, mostly about a missing lady named Agnes.

"Is this a wedding party?" asked the younger of the two men as his party stopped at the only other table. He stared at Timarie.

"Married just this afternoon," I affirmed. I didn't want any wandering thoughts that they had stumbled on a jilted bride and her father.

"Mind if we join you," asked the same man, who introduced himself as David Byrne, his eyes still fixed on Timarie.

"Please do," I said, beckoning the barkeep-deskwoman who was already on her way.

The balance of the introductions were made. The lady, *très distingué*, straight-spined and in her mid-sixties, was the Countess Pashkoff, of Vence, in Southern France; the other man was Bob Johnson of New York, well-dressed and appearing to be in his healthy late sixties, slow-speaking brother to the Countess and husband to the missing Agnes, who was described as off being busy with some duty or other that redounded to her as one of the prime movers of the Yeats International Summer School.

"Can I photograph you?" David Byrne asked Timarie, fingering the neckstrap of his Nikon. His stare repeatedly went back to her, after making perfunctory eye-contact with the rest of us.

"Of course," Timarie said. She was flattered. While David stood on his chair, then ranged a full semi-circle around us to get his proper camera angles, the Countess quizzed Timarie in American on the wedding particulars. Bob had broken into a constant smile and faintly uttered approving sounds like "uuhhh" and "hoooom."

"Did you have a hat?" the Countess asked Timarie.

"Yes, it's in my room." I could tell by Timarie's short answers that she was taken with the Countess.

"Then go get it," the Countess ordered in her well-mannered way.

"Do," David echoed. "I'd like to photograph you in it if I may."

While the obliging Timarie went upstairs to get her chapeau, I engaged the newest Mr. Byrne in talk. No, he was no relation to Kieran. "Just an early retired medical doctor from Dublin who's become a full-time student of Irish literature is all," he confided coyly.

My pilgrimage flared with renewed zeal. What Yeats poems were his favorites? What did *he* think Yeats' place was in Irish literature? What about James Joyce?

Byrne deftly sidestepped my sophomoric question on favorite poems. He did say that Joyce deserved more attention than he was getting. That there were at least two major branches of modern Irish literature, that of Yeats and Synge with its established cachet, and the more neglected strain of Joyce and O'Casey, which was ripe for more festivalizing.

Then Timarie returned, glowing under a faint blush, round cream hat in place, bouquet in hand, and Byrne went avidly back to his camera action, answering my questions almost offhandedly as he weaved and shot. At first I felt hurt. He said his hobby was literature, not photography. But it didn't take long for me to wake up. A close look at Timarie, shining on the day she had wanted and so brilliantly planned, did it. The photographer saw her beauty on her day. Not mine or Yeats' or Joyce's or Bob's or the Countess Pashkoff's, but Tim's time in the sun that, alas, *is* young once only.

The drinks were drunk. The chicken sandwiches were a residue of small crumbs. Bob reminded his party that Agnes was probably waiting. Time for another parting.

The Countess graciously invited us to visit her in Vence. I told her we would try some day, and—though she probably didn't think we would and might be alarmed if it became a future fact—I meant it; I hadn't been to that splendid artists' place in 16 years, but it remains my favorite town in Europe.

"Ireland owns its words and its poets," Dr. Bryne, as though compensating for and summing up a fragmentary lecture more understood than heard, said to me as we shook hands. "They all come home...or take home with them like an unshakable burden."

"Even Samuel Beckett?" I asked of his departing back.

Doctor Byrne stopped suddenly and spun on his heels. He peered at me in a different, more respectful way, as though there might have been some worthy pub gab sacrificed this late Monday afternoon when he chose to spend his time taking pictures of a young bride, who only incidentally and probably by irrelevant accident happened to be my wife. "Even him! Samuel Beckett will come back to Ireland, in his person or in his soul, before the end." Exit together the Doctor and the Countess and Bob.

A subdued Father Dave joined us for dinner in the hotel dining room. Repair costs to his car had exceeded his expectations. He had no money left to pay for dinner. My treat, I insisted. That was the least I could do for a man and priest who did so much to make a girl-in-her-prime's prime dream come true. For the second night in a row I ordered the local salmon, cold. No, not for any alleged priapic powers. Because Ireland's Atlantic salmon not only is less filling...it also tastes great!

From the false balcony of the Ballincar's bridal suite, we watched above the spacious front lawn's sleeping sheep a small string of late-twilight lamps glimmer along the reach toward Rosses Point. Life anywhere out there could not be sweeter than it was where we stood.

A knock on the door broke the reverie.

I answered it. The smiling maid handed me the ice bucket Tim had ordered to chill the wedding-night champagne.

"Thanks." I turned to Timarie. "You want to do the honors?"

"Sure." Timarie picked up the green box labeled Dom Perignon. I fetched the two bathroom tumblers. Funny, I thought. Here's a prized product fermented in France, shipped all the way to California, and then lugged aboard airplanes and carted around in a car, unloaded each night and

157

loaded each morning to almost double back, to reach this distant northern shore to salute the rarest of occasions.

Timarie slid two fingers the seal, broke it and pulled out the magnum. "Korbel" read the label. I was wrong. The juice and the switch had a California origin.

"Let's not bother," Timarie said through half a smile.

"Right. It deserves the round-trip budget rate."

I am pleased to immodestly report the rest of the night improved quickly and dramatically.

The video goes into rewind. The pictures are put away. Some lines of T. S. Eliot invade my mind:

> There is a time for the evening under starlight,
> A time for the evening under lamplight
> (The evening with the photograph album)
> Love is most nearly itself
> When here and now cease to matter.

# August 17    *Another Pendulum Swing*

Molly gets a stroller ride on this sunny California Sunday as Timarie joins us for the daily walk, two-plus miles through our neighborhood. I have to bend my back at an awkward and hurtful angle when pushing the stroller (I prefer the Napsak), while Mom not only is the right height, but takes the time to arrange several rolled receiving blankets to prop her daughter into an upright position.

Our route includes a pass by one of the city's rent-a-plot vegetable gardens, where a tomato plant has poked a major branch through the chain-link fence and brought forth a bumper crop that careless feet will soon puree on the sidewalk. Timarie gets a bag from a 7-Eleven across the street, and I fill it with about two pounds of fresh ripe cherry tomatoes—an addition to tonight's salad, with many to spare.

Molly's hunger cry begins before we arrive at our front door. While Tim scrambles to ready herself for the breast-feeding (including a hot-water rinse to prevent a recurrence of the breast infection), I do my schtick. With nothing else but my friendly features and my patter of baby talk, I'm able to transform the puckered face into a happy face for 57 seconds—until chow arrives. Another one for the *Guinness Book of World Records.*

Timarie says, "That girl really loves you."

"You think so?"

"Look, if that were me holding her, she wouldn't tolerate anything this long. When she sees me it's 'Feed me now.' With you she knows you're going to take care of her—play with her. She relies on me because I'm the food person. Her love for you is more a voluntary love."

"The pendulum swings back and forth," I say consolingly.

"I want the pendulum to stop. I want us to all love each other the same."

# August 18   *A Day Of Suffering*

Why did I ever do it? Become a parent again. This is among the most maddening, exhausting days of my life. Molly is fussing and crying non-stop. Why? I'm feeding her enough. Is it the heat? It's in the mid-90s and muggy, but there have been other hot days....Is she thirsty? No, the water offered is contemptuously refused. Gas? No, she always has gas. Then she scares the wits out of me by choking on what I think must be some crumb that somehow made its errant way into her mouth. No, it's her tongue, which she's discovered is something she can chew on. Gum on, I mean.

The crying is endless and nothing can stop it. Her walker pleases her not, the swing brings angry complaints, her cradle is a prison for venting her rage, which now includes thrusting her butt in the air and really belting out some down-home, red-headed anger.

It worsens during the children's hour. I move her to the living room floor where I've spread a blanket and brought her Three Men in a Tub. The poor old Candlestickmaker is immediately sent flying across the room with a hostile swipe. Why won't she sleep? What the hell am I going to do?

In an inspired moment I turn on the television, to the Dodger game. She quiets, wide-open eyes fixed on the screen. Fantastic! The magic of baseball again! For about eight minutes, which is as long as her arms can prop up her chest and head. When the head strikes the blanket again the crying reaches new heights in frustration. Even when I pick her up and hold her, she whines and thrashes in my arms.

When Timarie gets home I make the transfer with a desperate "She's all yours."

"A bad day?"

"The worst."

At 8:20 p.m. I stagger into bed alone to collapse in utter exhaustion. A few minutes later Timarie brings Molly in and lays her down beside me. "I think she's tired, too."

"Yeah. Thanks a lot."

## August 19   *A Sore For Sighted Eyes*

Start off each day with a smile. Right, at 6:16 a.m. Forgive and forget, Molly beams. How wonderful that children are reborn each morning, energized by their young protoplasm. Pity that this life juice stales over time.

On the negative side of the ledger, and maybe one reason for yesterday's cranking, Molly has come down with cradle cap. Also called, by me, cradle crap or head crud. Ugly, crusty patches underlie her thin red hair, caused, I read, by newborns' not having sufficient hair to absorb the natural oils secreted by scalp glands. So lint and dirt cling and coalesce into an unsightly condition that is not serious but makes you want to hide the kid from public eyes.

The heat, down to the low-90s today, may be the culprit, but Molly and I meet it frontally with a 2:00-p.m., three-mile, errandless walk through our neighborhood. I notice Molly staring at the ground as we go, and for a while I can't make out what it is that's fascinating her. Then I see. It's our shadows in motion...the black-and-white contrast again.

Each day seems to bring one new revelation or thing done by my little girl. Today there's a second. When Timarie calls from work to say she'll be late for dinner, I hold up the phone to Molly's ear to hear her mother's voice. A jungfrau beetlebrow look, then a smile that I'll swear is one of recognition.

# August 20   *A Child Forming*

Cradle cap's all gone and the sunny smiles are back on my girl of the morning. Mom "cured" it. Last night she rubbed baby oil into Molly's scalp, then let it soak in all night. Early this morning Timarie brushes the gummy flakes out of Molly's hair with a soft-bristled brush, follows it with a thorough shampoo, and, presto!—crud's no more.

My daughter's restored good humor extends to all but the Candlestickmaker this morning. Poor devil gets abandoned again as she grabs and fondles, drops and retrieves, the pure white Baker and the yellow, black-mustachioed Butcher. What does she have against red, O-mouthed, pointy-headed candlestickmakers? When I try to intrude on her play and push the guy on her, he catches a dismissing back of the hand that sends him sprawling. Molly goes back to Butcher and Baker with single-mindedness.

Single-mindedness, yes, the word's appropriate. There's another that probably should go with it to describe this infant girl whose personality I think I see forming. She's stubborn. I could color it and say determined, but hey! Let's face it . . . she may be determined but she's also stubborn. And hot-tempered, befitting her hair color. Anger. Yes, strangely, it seems to me, that emotion is firmly fixed in her repertoire. It's shown most when I put her into her crib before she's ready. Her tiny bottom rises in the air in protest. And when I wind up her one-bird-on-a-rainbow-swing mobile that plays, rather touchingly, I think, "Somewhere Over the Rainbow," she chews her fist in rage, partially choking off bitter cries that seem to charge me—me personally!—with betrayal. Yes, my daughter is growing up.

I should add that the word humming through the nearer-than-local grapevine is "spoiled." As in "Molly is spoiled." Now, how the hell can that be?! How can you spoil a baby not yet three months old? Spoiling as I define it means the unwarranted giving to a child needless things and false expectations. It has nothing to do with lavishing attention and affection on one new to the race. Who would deny a newborn the courtesy of that beginning?

With no other credentials than being on my fourth child at an advanced age, I say sin on the side of doting and stroking, not of striking and neglect.

# August 21     *Close Call*

I write this in the journal to remind myself and all parents of infants what we all know and yet still don't always act on.

Never, never, never leave a baby unattended.

Never, never, never underestimate what they are capable of doing physically. Their abilities—motor and otherwise—grow daily and prodigiously.

At nine this morning I have Molly in her infant seat atop the dining room table, about four feet off the floor. Timarie walks by and says, "I wouldn't put her up there—she might fall."

I agree. But when I return from our afternoon hike, I again temporarily deposit her in the infant seat, this time on the living room floor, while I go to the kitchen to make a sandwich.

It takes me a few seconds to identify the cry I hear as one of distress. I rush into the room to find Molly's infant seat overturned and the baby trembling on the carpet, head just an inch from an oak leg of the coffee table. Oh thank God for the near-miss! And thank God I hadn't left her on top of the dining room table.

At 5:15 I have Molly in the infant seat again. This time safely belted in beside me as I drive to pick up Timarie, then a six-pack of Heineken and a big bag of potato chips. My business cards and stationery are ready to be picked up, and we're going to celebrate the happy day with John and Kean, the two young men who have just started their own ad agency and for whom I'm either the first or second client. It's a small world, even in populous Southern California. Kean was on the Fall '83 staff of the college magazine I advise, John—then an art major at CSULB—created the front cover for the following spring's issue. Now the three of us have come together a few years later, largely by chance, to celebrate our mutual ventures into the business world, as well as the opening of their brand new office, K. Wesley Hall Advertising.

"To success!" Kean says as he hoists his Heineken high. We all join in the toast, save Molly, who is nonetheless fascinated by these adult goings on and stares at Kean from her mother's lap.

"See you at the top!" Kean adds.

"At the top!" I echo, mindful that, unlike the others, I may have already reached my zenith, at least in the commercial world. Certainly toting my infant daughter to a homey beer-and-potato-chip happy hour would be commonly thought a big slip in status from those old three-martini lunches on Wilshire Boulevard when I was a magazine editor. Yet I find it a congenial slip, and the company better.

At home Timarie and I retreat to the patio with Molly to catch the sunset.

"Why don't I serve dinner out here?"

"Good idea."

I bring it to the patio table—homemade chili and soda crackers.

"Ummmm!" Timarie allows as she leans over lapbound Molly to lick clean her spoon. "I think this is the best chili you've ever made."

# August 22     *The Scapegoat*

Five straight days in a row, if you can believe that. Five successive times Molly forcibly jettisoned the Candlestickmaker from the tray of her walker, keeping the Butcher and Baker for cuddling. What are the odds of that happening randomly, you lizards of Las Vegas?

Well, the sample is still too small for me to even begin positing any world-jolting conclusion, like bigotry being inborn, not learned. Why, I'd be packed off to science's leper colony in no time to join the likes of Lysenko!

At 5:24 p.m., after fussing in her cradle for 40 minutes, I bring a crying Molly in beside me as I hack at the wordprocessor. And she continues her crying. Until I mug and babytalk her into a smile. Maybe it is the angle of her looking up, the facial tilt, maybe the way her hair was brushed that raised the wave and back curls, the taper of her chin, but I see the spitting image of myself, as recorded in the only baby picture I have of myself below age two.

A stump roots in my throat. "You're my daughter...you're my daughter."

The words rush out as a half-laugh, half-sob, and that startles me. Tears have taken my eyes. Red alert at Chernobyl.

She stares at me with the beginnings of human wonder.

In any case, we're related.

# August 23     *Conception*

At 6:57 a.m. I'm at the Kaypro, an alert Molly at my side, playing not with the Butcher, not with the Baker, and of course not the Candlestickmaker, but with her limber "Traffic Light," a recent gift from Tim's friend Teresa. This little marvel, an import from England, supports on the vertical plastic stanchion three plastic "lights" with bead rattles in them and connects via a rubber suction cup to the tray top of her walker. I know it won't be long before she stops batting the thing back and forth, before its rattling innards go silent, before her patience gives out and she starts to cry. Hard to believe that my Molly Margaret—this one-of-a-self girl who would by cosmic plan or our earthly choice enter the small minority of possible human beings ever to draw breath—began one year ago today....

Saturday was a Friday then, and at this time of the mid-morning the day's love was over, Timarie sleeping beside me as I watched footage of the morning's Liverpool air crash on British television news, thinking how ironic it would be if, at this time of mass death, we joined sex cells this first time....That on the first post-nuptial fertile cycle...on the first try, on West Cromwell Road, Tim would conceive a largely Celtic-kraut Catholic child on West Cromwell Road....44-46 West Cromwell Road, South Kensington. (Take that, you Roundhead butcher!)

Of course it could have been the previous morning, or the evening before that, Wednesday, the day after we limped in from Paris, off the hydrofoil, barf-bags in hand. Wednesday night to Friday morning—those were the 48 hours when the race would be stacked in favor of the slower, longer-enduring sperm bearing X chromosomes. After this Friday morning there could be no more finished love for days...at least four more days but preferably more, when we knew, through reading and daily temperature charting, the odds would shift quickly and dramatically in the favor of the smaller, swifter-but-short-lived Y-bearing sperm.

I had talked Timarie out of her hesitancy. Why wait? For me a bad policy. And what if we connected? The baby would be born in late May, just as the semester was ending, and our widened family would have a whole summer together, to bond. Yes, the plan.

August 23...the only leisurely day on Project London Drama Overdose...six plays in four days—utter madness, but planned madness.

Timarie woke at 11:00 angry that I had let her sleep through most of her assigned shopping time at Harrods. My saying I thought she needed the rest she believed disingenuous, a mask for my usual anti-shopping strategies. My lukewarm protests of innocence cut no ice...so we walked through Mayfair in a slight chill...then we warmed some as we trod on to Covent Garden, where over a late lunch on a gray day we watched a knot of bizarrely attired punkers shake-down a well-dressed black American tourist they had cleverly allowed to take pictures before claiming and collecting model fees. We had to rush by tube back to the hotel to dress for the night's play at the National Theatre, a revival of *She Stoops to Conquer*...an augury there? Well, I wouldn't try to read it.

Buoyed by Goldsmith's wit, we crossed Waterloo Bridge arm-in-arm, walked through ragged lines of spent drunks to a Thames-side stand, where we bought and shared a greasy but tasty plaice wrapped in newspaper, with soggy chips. By the time we'd tubed back to West Cromwell Road, the possibilities of the morning had left our minds.

Odd how, when you're traveling, the present shoulders past and future aside, frees the mind and senses to seek out and adapt to the unfamiliar. The weekend hurried us to a *Hamlet* matinee at the Barbican, to Pinter-directed *Sweet Bird of Youth* at the Haymarket, to my midnight scuffle in a subway car braking at the Picadilly Circus stop, a shoving match with a pickpocket who—perish the thought!—almost made off with Timarie's purse and our passports; a Sunday morning lark in the park among Hyde Park's hecklers and orators, gently negotiating for tee-shirts and antique type with the sidewalk hawkers in Saint James's Park; the great luck of happening upon a late-afternoon concert in Westminster Abbey, with pre-Bach booming harmonies from a huge old pipe organ stirring the comforting and humbling and exalting and saddening properties of soul. All that while, some 200 million sperm cells probably made the race, about 50 reached the waiting egg, and only one had penetrated it to line up its chromosomes with those of the giant hostess in yet another unique genetic pairing. Over that same span, the parent cell had already divided, perhaps twice for a total of four...the miraculous acceleration of another life toward birth.

Monday morning comes and, wander as they might, it's mostly plumbing that sends Americans back where they came from. Neither of us really gave it much thought during the TWA jet's long 11-hour afternoon polar flight that we might be taking a new life home with us.

# August 24    *Nix On My Three Tubbers Theory*

Molly sees herself in the mirror the first time this morning and smiles. Does she recognize herself in the glass? And like what she sees? I hope so, because that would mean she approves of herself, and that's the right way to start a life.

Molly also demolishes my nascent theory of the innate nature of bigotry with two sweeps of her little arm. Fresh from her mid-morning nap and into the walker, on the front tray of which I've placed the Three Men in a Tub for her sorting, she sends the Butcher and Baker reeling across the floor, then pulls the Candlestickmaker to her drool-drenched shirtfront, before extending him to a bent arm's length and gumming his pointy red head. There goes my big splash in the research pond and probably my Nobel Prize in Psychology as well. Yes, the scientific method is a rigorous one, not easy on us glory-seekers. But then again, does one deviation from a rigid pattern of five necessarily mean I have to scrap the whole theory? Maybe she just got momentarily bored with the two good guys and wanted to inspect the one dressed in red close up.

Closer to the truth is that a new favorite toy, just arrived from the toy-of-the-month-club, has supplanted the tubsters and the stoplight. To my first and second and third glance—no, make that inspection—the Wiggle Worm made an unlikely candidate for her playtime. Pieces of yellow, green, and red fabric patched onto an ungainly and unlikely fish-shaped creature, with big black button eyes that when squeezed make a wheezy unwormlike sound, and a series of three blue plastic rings (teething rings, it turns out) where the ventral fins would be, if it were a fish, which I still think it more nearly resembles. A silly-looking miniature monster that no self-respecting baby would play with.

Molly strokes it, rubs it, gums it, cries when she drops it from her walker tray, needs it by her pillow when we put her in the crib at night, and fondles it contentedly when she's in the car seat.

I probably don't have much of a future in the toy business.

Future.

Odd how that word bothers me now. Most of my life I've spent Janus-like, looking back to a past bittersweet with good times and failures, and forward with hope and the resolve to make something of myself. The present never amounted to more than standing ground for facing fore and aft.

Not now. Even at this moment, 3:04 p.m., with Molly napping and me at the kitchen sink scrubbing her bottles and nipples with one of the three brushes Timarie has bought for the job (she'll inspect my work, too, and I'll feel the heat if proper standards of sterility are not maintained), I favor the present.

Why the turnabout? I'm not sure. Perhaps because Molly has so much future and I have so much less, and the two may not overlap long.

# August 25     *Supermarket Self-Defense*

At Vons this morning I get both barrels. First a guy near the dented can bin looks at my Napsak, where Molly's red head bounces like one of those dashboard dolls, and says, "Is that your grand—"

"No, it's my daughter," I cut him off.

Volley two comes at the checkout stand, where I'm most vulnerable, trying to juggle Molly, a checkbook, wallet for identification and unused store coupons, all before a small audience.

"You got a granddaughter there?" asks a guy behind me in line who definitely looks like a grandfather.

"No, it's my daughter," I say, nimbly adding, "my late-in-life blessing for having been such a splendid fellow all my life." Laughs around at my inspired defense. I intend to have the words cocked and ready for firing at the next reference to my age.

Molly was such a good baby at the store. But as soon as I get her in the house and try to put her down, she lets loose with a new cry that I can only call piercing. She is flat-out sleep-resistant, as were my previous three children. None of them ever wanted to yield consciousness any more than I did...or do. I have no doubt that if I were selectively bred to a like female, we would produce stock that four generations hence would get along on 45 minutes of sleep a day—and be tucked away in the loony bin before turning 30.

Fortunately, my young wife is of a different metabolism. She reveres sleep, appreciates its recuperative value, celebrates its intrinsic beauty.

# August 26  *Looking Forward*

One week till all this must end is the sad thought I wake to today. Each recent day has been a blossom day, when Molly makes at least one great leap forward in her development. Her face is animated as never before, and she bestows smiles on most everyone she meets, in stores or on the street.

I am happy this early a.m. because Molly is happy at my side, tiptoeing around in her walker, gumming her Wiggle Worm.

Could she be teething? Who's to know? I've read in Leach that babies don't start until five or six months old, and Molly is just over three. She must just be exploring her world, her way. I'm thankful. It buys me an hour-plus of writing time.

I am so happily abstracted that I boo-boo when I change her and forget to put on the plastic (I keep calling them *rubber* from the last round) pants; so she pees in her Pilucho, then cries. Writing time surrenders to child-care time.

"Molly is not a baby, she's a person," Timarie announces as she dresses for work. "She's always been."

I think about it. Yes. How many of us pay lip service to the idea but really think of our infant children as extensions of ourselves—or helpless, ignorant blobs totally dependent on us?

Molly is indeed a person, but since she lives inside a body that won't yet let her tell us her thoughts and feelings, it's hard to know her in all her complexity. More and more I allow myself to think of her as a future person... in different situations, at different ages. Vaporous thoughts, because it's not long before I either find that I've been projecting what *I* want her to be in that future, or the situation itself is subtly disturbing.

"Have you ever thought of her as an adult?" Timarie asks, as though reading my mind.

"Yes."

"How? Doing what?"

"Oh... as a college girl... a chaser of truth... a doer of great deeds."

"Even as a lover?"

"A little bit... in the abstract. I don't take it far."

"As a mother?"

"That more often."

"How does that strike you?" Tim's eyes attach to my face.

"Glad...and sad."

"Glad that she'll experience what it's like being a mother?"

"Yes. That. Fulfillment."

"Any other reason?"

"Well...it would mean I'd have a grandchild. That would be nice...carrying on the strain, lengthening the line." I don't want Timarie to ask me why Molly's motherhood might make me sad, but I expect it...momentarily.

She doesn't. Apparently her mind is still tracking mine. There's no need to feed my thanatophobia and my nagging fear that I will never live to see Molly with a child of her own. It comes with our unconventional match. And it doesn't have to be discussed to death...or very often at all.

"Molly's been here before," Tim says with a detached certainty.

I do not answer. Her mind has made a great leap forward. I follow, but I don't tell her. I don't have to. She believes in immortality, a recurrence of being—if not an out-and-out blissful afterlife, in which she and I and Molly will be reunited for all eternity. She knows me as the infidel arch-skeptic, ruined by a few UCLA philosophy courses that pushed radical empiricism. Have faith, she is saying.

But now, at 9:11 a.m., it's off to work she goes.

At 1:10 p.m., after Molly's bottle, as I putter at cleaning in the kitchen, I turn to check her in her walker chair. A sudden numbing jolt. My eyes see, in the peaches and cream, heart-shaped face beneath the copper thatch, my mother. Not just a physical resemblance between Molly and the one baby picture I have of my mother...that's been noted before. But the sense of my mother's presence in the child...in the eyes that encompass me.

My radical empiricism may be weakening. And I like it.

# August 27  *Ghosts And Whispers*

A routine day of diaper swaps and measurings-out of Isomil cut equally with pumped-and-frozen-and-thawed plastic bags of breast milk leads to an evening that, for reasons not quite clear to me, I've strangely got the jitters for.

Timarie wants Molly baptized three weeks hence in the Catholic Church by Father Dave, the priest who married us in Ireland. All quite right and fitting, though his parish is about 30 miles distant, in Pico Rivera, a predominantly Hispanic community I know from a boyhood spent in adjacent Whittier. That means a long round-trip with Molly on a hot night for a dress rehearsal...well, religious instruction, really.

Hot gets hotter in the church's small stuccoed annex, where some 30 adults and half that number of fussing infants assemble in what seems a classroom to hear Father Dave speak on the meaning of baptism and parental and god-parental responsibilities within the Faith. The questions he asks are mostly rhetorical, and audience tension relaxes noticeably when he answers the harder ones himself.

Not ten minutes into the lesson and the perspiration is rolling off the end of my nose in steady drips. I look to Molly, dressed in a pink terry-cloth jumper with a chicken that peeps when pressed sewn into the front; she continues to squirm uncomfortably in Timarie's arms and glistens with sweat. No doubt about it, as the pro-football broadcasters like to say, Molly has inherited my hyperactive cooling system, not Timarie's cool and dry look of being perpetually immersed in ice-blue Secret.

Molly begins to whine and cry, drawing even more general attention to the strange family at the right rear of the sweatroom. No wonder. Aside from Timarie's and my age difference, we are the only non-Hispanic couple in the room, and Molly, with her red hair and paler-than-pearl skin, is an interesting minority of one. The attention we get is not resentful...just curious.

Father Dave is kind, and mercifully condenses the lesson. Then, at lecture's end, smiling under his usual blushing cheeks, he approaches us for the first time, studying, with seeming detachment, the infant whose legitimacy he presided over.

"So it's Molleen O'Houlihan, is it!" he says in his deepest brogue. The red hair seems to puzzle him. I want to explain that it came from my mother, but before the first greetings have subsided he is surrounded with parishioners. It takes me some minutes of careful listening to determine that their business is more important than mine. Seems some of the young parents who have brought their children for baptizing have not themselves been blessed in matrimony, so, while it's convenient, the prerequisite sacrament should be performed...putting everything right, as it were. La Vida finds no paradox here, and who's to say it should?

It's hot still—the hottest night of the year—and Molly cries and whines when we reach the car for the drive home.

"Why don't you sit in the back with her," Timarie suggests. "See if you can comfort her."

Agreed, though it's additional weight on my weary, flagging spirit. Driving down Whittier Boulevard, Molly's fuss continues, despite my tries at amusing her.

Up the south onramp of the 605 Freeway...an easy merge into remarkably open lanes...and into the night vision I remember from early childhood of sudden light and sudden shadow from roadside stanchions, into the interstitial fade to gloom and blurring shadow, only to brighten both quickly and predictably in the glow of another light, a visual rhythm that invariably turned me inward as a child and suddenly, naturally, does again, now.

Miraculously, it seems to me, Molly ceases crying and latches onto my eyes with hers. They change, age, become instantly understanding of something beyond either of us, far removed from this time and place. At first I don't break the lock because I don't want her to cry, but then I find myself won over to the eyes become wise...beyond wise.

Our stares stay fixed in dispassionate intimacy. A better word? Love. Yes, I would call it love...connecting my infant daughter with my 13-year-dead mother and me in a perfect triangle of...love. No other word remotely fits.

My rebellious forebrain keeps wanting to intrude, break the lock, analyze and explain away what is happening. From somewhere, or everywhere, in my body comes the will to fight back, hold onto this first-in-a-lifetime, euphoric feeling...of total peace...sublime love.

The timeless bond breaks with Molly suddenly, almost casually, turning her head to the exterior night. Over.

Twelve minutes. That's roughly the elapsed time I later reconstruct, based on the approximate 60-mph speed of Timarie's driving and the freeway miles between the last-remembered landmark before the onset of the trance and the place of my unwelcome return to the here and now.

My transcendent moments in life have been woefully few, perhaps because my mind won't let me deserve them. This interlude with Molly has been the finest of that few. Yes, I can analyze it "rationally." I admit that almost from the moment of her birth Molly has physically reminded me of my mother... in face cast, complexion, hair color. I am lately willing also to confront the great guilt I feel for deliberately avoiding my mother when she was on her deathbed, lingering in the hospital halls and with the doctors and undertaker when she was in her last hours. Why? Because I was too weak (though I've always used the word "considerate") to face her and have to possibly deny her the deathbed wish Stephen Dedalus so cruelly did to his mother. Yes, in this just-past tri-partite union, I feel she has finally forgiven me.

That may explain my part in the seance. But it sure doesn't explain Molly's.

# August 28    *Talking Baby*

This early morning, as Timarie holds out our beaming daughter, fresh from a diaper change, toward me, little Molly says "aba" (pronounced a-bah). The sound reaches out and back through some cerebral short circuit to my past, and I suddenly find myself conjugating out loud what ought to be a Latin verb if it isn't: "aba, abas, abat; abamus, abatis, abant."

Timarie looks at me blankly and asks for an explanation, then approves when I tell her of my reflex act that dated back to my high school sophomore Latin class. "Approves" might seem an odd choice of word. But I don't think so. Our verbal anarchy and nonsense word play in the presence of Molly isn't—or maybe wasn't is the better word—always shared. For the first month-plus we were not comfortable with each other's babytalk.

I suspect the same is true of other new parents. One's own products are tolerable, even satisfying, while those of others are almost always offensive. You doubt? Think of that last gut-turning time in the supermarket checkout line when you were subjected to a precious "oo-goo-sugar-bunny-bunkins" exchange between a tot-toting young mother customer and a nostalgic, middle-aged inactive mother member of the Retail Clerks Union. Picture the expression on your face—the one you couldn't hide.

I know Timarie's first terms of endearment for Molly set me back, if they didn't put me off. For instance, "Badorna," with the accent on the middle syllable. What the hell does that mean? Or "Punkinorska?" Or "Punkinina?" Or its contraction to the long-used "Nina?"—an irritant to me because it reduced her to a generic girl-child.

Timarie was more tolerant of my early smarm-nouns for Molly, such as "Bourdon," which Mom liked for its French sound, but which actually owed its derivation to my calling my first-generation set of sons "bird-heads" after their bobbing bald pates in cribs at feeding time; in time bird-head went to bird-dome and finally, with Molly, the corruption to "Bourdon," which just sounded better. I also called her early "Dolleena" (sung "Dollena, Dollena," to the tune of "Corinna, Corinna"), which degenerated to "Squawleena" under the natural pressures of baby needs wedded to onomatopoeia.

Other early sobriquets were "Dollheart II" (which Dollheart I had identified two years earlier as not being all that flattering to human females) and 'Sugar Booger'—not the crude slavery to assonance it might seem, since the name belonged to a fine-sprinting filly who used to burn the Santa Anita strip a couple of generations back.

It's 9:37 a.m. Timarie has gone to work, Molly to bed for her morning nap, and I am at the keyboard to finish this necessary confession—or just to get down for Molly's future sake the other terms of endearment I've lavished on her. There's "Tiny Heart," in part after the shape of her head, but which has had its successor in "Little Heart," which evolved, on a parallel-then-joining track of "You Cute," "You Cuter," and the diminutive "Cutarita," into my favorite spondee of all, "Cute-Heart."

There are also etymological dead-ends, such as the much-favored "Happy Heart," the associative wandering of "Little Heart on the Prairie," or "Molliko," to move her to the Japan of my young manhood, or into such nonsensical associative phrases sung or jingled.. ."Good Golly, Miss Molly, It's only Gully Jimpson," or—beyond associative reach—"Yes, Yes a Doodle Dandy, I'm that Molly Doodle Girl," shrilly sung to the old song, of course, sounding not unlike what you'd hear from an unprimed hen with quinsy being violated.

And then the life-death-loop-to-love manifest these last three weeks in my calling her "Pooperton," after her many (or so it seems to me) bowel movements, borrowed from the late Prunella Pimperton (whose many droppings I've come to miss scooping up from the back lawn). Pooperton, in turn gives way to Pinkerton, erupting from the mouth when I first see Molly in her pink fleece sleeper with the little-bear applique over the heart—my little Pink Bear of the Prairie and the Cute Heart who filled more than the void left by a little black dog.

Why all this mushy gushing that's enough to gag even your average flower-shop clerk? I wish I really knew, little Molly Marg, but it's heartfelt in any case. I'd like to tell you there's an inner music and meaning in our rhythmic grunts and silly gabble; that the pleasure we take from the music of sounds before words leads into making words, and words in turn lead to our understanding and appreciating God's great plan.

But I don't know that. Maybe the value of the sounds is only in their being shared, wonderful but inadequate ways of bridging our lives. Beyond that, it may be that our delight in mere sound mirrors nothing more than the random nonsense of the universe.

And so the thoughts go at the computer this morning.

# August 29   *Someone Who Will Care*

The new semester looms, only a few days away. This is Convocation Day, when the President gives his "state of the university" speech, after which the School of Humanities meets with its Dean for more developments and directions, and then the department meets to discuss immediate matters—most of them anticipated problems.

All this will take two-thirds of a day and means Molly must be cared for...for the first time by a non-family, professional child-carer who lives 2.8 miles out of my way on the drive to school, as I find on this morning trial-run of things to come. I feel both tongue-tied and uneasy when I drop Molly off with her Igloo full of breastmilk/formula mix, her diaper-bag stuffed with garments and ointments and toys, and her infant car seat. I'm numb at the prospect of not having Molly with me today, even though Cathy, a woman in her early fifties who is both mother and grandmother several times over, takes the baby from me with practiced care and gentleness.

Timarie, acting on a reference by a sister, selected Cathy after a lengthy personal interview and several phone conversations. She would correct me and say "we" selected her, because she insisted I be present at the interview. I did muddle my way through the two hours of paptalk, feeling an outsider for the first time in a long time, and that baby care was probably not meant to be my life's work. Maybe it was simply a matter of no experience on my part. My first family was raised before it became necessary that both parents (in all but wealthy families, of course) work outside of the home. This professional child-care idea was all so new, and, I suspect, so depressing deep down.

Timarie in her customary thoroughness had a checklist of things to ask and things to look for in the house. I put them down here because they could be helpful.

Start by checking local, state or county licensing agencies for referrals. (They are often listed by ZIP code, so you can tell whether they are close to your home or work.) Stay with licensed sitters—unless you have friends or family in mind. Then interview them, preferably in the company of the baby you want them to sit; see if the baby-sitter automatically takes the child from your arms as though she can't wait to hold it. Does she seem comfortable and confident? How does the baby react? You can pick up some valuable emotional fall-out from this encounter before you ask your first question.

"Are your hours flexible?"

If the sitter is very rigid about drop-off and pick-up hours, and you have a variable work schedule, do yourself a favor and scratch the candidate off your list. A baby-sitter with inflexible hours probably won't have time to chat at pick-up time, when you want to be filled-in on how your child spent her day. How did she eat? When and how long did she sleep? How does she behave around other children? What is she learning? Does she need more food?

"How many children do you baby-sit now?"

Licensed sitters will be limited in the number they can mind at the same time. Six is the number in our area (for one without an assistant), and that can be too many to insure proper care.

"What are the ages of the children you sit?"

Mixing infants with toddlers and also older preschoolers can be good, or bad. It poses problems with sleeping schedules, risks eye-pokings, minor body bruises, and so forth. On the other hand, your child is likely to learn more, faster, with other, older kids around.

"Do you prefer any age group? What are the age limits on the children you sit?"

Some sitters will only mind infants. Others prefer older children. Be sure your child fits into the preferred group and isn't considered an afterthought. And if the sitter minds only infants, keep in mind that you will need to find another when the child turns three or so...start over, in effect.

"How many children of your own do you have? Did you have?"

Older women who have raised families and have reached that "grandmotherly age" are often prime choices—experienced and caring. You, of course, should communicate all your apprehensions and doubts up-front, without insulting the candidate, who is likely to have her own opinions on child-rearing based on more experience than you possess.

"How long have you been baby-sitting?"

Duration generally means experience and a liking for the job, and therefore is a plus.

"What did you do before you baby-sat?"

Not an off-the-wall question.... The answer can reveal a lack of experience and/or background and attitudes that may either please you or eliminate the person as a candidate.

"Are you married? What does your husband do? How many people live in the house? Are there times during the day when you must leave the house? If so, who minds the children?"

These might be thought prying questions, but it is your child's well-being that's at stake. Phrase your questions both agreeably and aggressively. And get answers. When you do get close to making a choice, insist on meeting everyone in the family. Pick a day when they'll all be at home. Say something like, "Would your family be able to meet with me and my husband (wife) this weekend?"

"Did you breast-feed your children? If so, for how long?"

(Because Timarie is committed to that womanly art, those who share her feelings on the subject are automatically simpatico and raised in candidacy.)

"Are you willing to use cloth diapers?"

Some sitters aren't. Pampers, Luvs, Huggies, etc. are easier—especially when several children are being sat—and the danger of safety pins is removed. On the other hand, there are times and reasons (diaper rashes, related skin problems) when and why cotton diapers that breathe should be used. Clear the matter up now.

"Do you have any pets?"

You have a right to know what they are, where they are kept, and judge whether they pose any danger to your child. Allergies to cats and dogs are common enough; do you know how your baby reacts to them?

"Does any one in the household smoke?"

The health threat—particularly to infants—of second-hand smoke is a documented fact. Why expose your child?

"What is your policy on sick babies?"

This policy cuts both ways—for you and against you. It also raises a number of questions that should be raised and answered, even if those answers fail to resolve the larger issue of what you do with a sick child. Some sitters will not mind a child with a fever over 100 degrees. This should please you if your baby is not the afflicted one; you don't want every bug brought into the sitter's house carried home to yours. But what if it *is* your child? Do you have back-up care somewhere? Are you prepared (can you afford?) to stay home and mind the baby? When your baby becomes sick at the sitter's, will she call you to come and pick her up? Some sitters will not accept a child that has just had a DPT shot; they do not want to be liable in case of adverse reactions. Discuss all these contingencies ahead of time, so there are no harsh surprises later.

Is the house baby-safe? Check carefully the rooms in which the children are kept. Look for exposed sharp edges on furniture and fireplaces, glass objects within reach—especially when toddlers are sat. Inspect the area where the children sleep. Observe the condition of the house. Is it a chaotic mess, suggesting a lack of organizing skills? Is it immaculate? (Not necessarily a good sign either, because who is minding the children when all that housework is being done?)

When you're pretty close to making your final choice, ask for references. Get one parent currently sat for and one for a child no longer sat. Explore any doubts you have with the references.

Turn the tables. Ask the prospective sitter or sitters if they have any questions of *you*. They might...and in any case will appreciate your openness—your willingness to discuss things candidly. And that will pay dividends later when the child is being cared for.

Bring up money last. Licensed sitters generally have government-set or sanctioned rates, which may or may not be negotiable. Clear up payment policies for sickness (when the child stays home with you), holidays and family vacations—yours, and theirs, if any. Try to set the terms if you can, but be prepared to be told you must pay full rate for sick days and holidays. The same may be true for vacations as well, though a half-rate compromise is possible. The rationale for paying for services you are not getting? The money reserves your space; otherwise the sitter's livelihood would depend on whether parents decided to bring their kids on any given day. As always, the laws of supply and demand intrude, and in locales of great demand good babysitters get mostly what they want. And who is to gainsay them that? Besides, you want the best for your baby.

After you've chosen a sitter and agreed on terms, don't just let the arrangement become one of routine drop-offs and pick-ups. Monitor the care your child is getting. Drop by unexpectedly during the day from time to time to see how it's going. Make time also to chat, so you can learn about your baby's progress. The sitter can be a fount of information and, as far as your baby is concerned, probably the most important person you will ever hire.

# August 30     *To A Precious Few*

**M**olly wakes crying in distress at 6:16 this morning. Once again, she has extended a limb—a leg this time, but in the past it's been an arm or one of each—under the cradle's bumper pads and got it caught between the slats. Getting too big for it. Soon she'll have to go to her crib, empty and waiting in her own room. Out of our sight.

Our daughter is showing a newly gained mastery of her hands. She shoves her fists in her mouth now at feeding time, and at the second one this morning, she clutches a diaper and stuffs that into her mouth, and Timarie has to fight her for it to clear the nipple's path.

Next it's bath time.

"Saturday, after all," say I.

Timarie, who bathes Molly every day and sees no humor in my words, dragged up from Norman Rockwell's America, mixes Molly's water to a just-right tepid temp taken with an elbow.

"You want me to hold her?" No, I'm too late. All is ready for the bath. So I tell Tim of yesterday's journal entry detailing her inquisition list, and how I think it might be helpful to other parents choosing babysitters.

"Well, if you're trying to be helpful, you might want to include my lists on choosing a hospital and selecting a pediatrician," she says.

"Already did the latter," I inform her.

Timarie lowers Molly into her yellow sponge-tub and begins a careful, small-area application of Dove soap and handcupped water rinses. Should I put the choosing-the-hospital list in? As an addendum? I don't know.

With a hooded baby towel, Tim dries Molly meticulously, even down to the final Q-tip-swirlings in the various recesses of her little ears.

"Is that really necessary?"

"Don't you dry your ears when you get out of the shower?"

I choose silence over the Fifth.

"You know that icky feeling when you don't? I put myself in her place."

"Yeah." A sop. Hell, she's my daughter. She can sleep in her poop without complaining...and does.

Tim starts dressing Molly in a fluffy, ill-fitting yellow sunsuit that I peg right off as a Dior-type fantasy. Why? Because Molly kicks and thrashes throughout the fitting, that's why. Still, Mom puts it on with greater deftness than dear old Dad could, I must admit.

Now the shoes. Little white Mary Janes that don't fit right. That's been my experience. "You'll have to unbuckle them first," I advise.

"No you don't."

The miniature feet get forced through minuscule slots. Molly bawls.

"We're going to get them on if we have to break your little ankles," I carp. I don't win many. But when I do, I revel in it.

Tim returns from her mother's with Molly at 5:20 p.m. They're both beat, but Molly vents her fatigue through crying. Fifteen minutes straight, without a break.

What's wrong? Overtired, yes, but also probably bored now that the day's doings are done.

I gather the little spider up and press her to my chest. She cries on. She also presses herself against me. I rub circles on her back with a hand that more than covers it. I kiss her tiny trembling face as I croon, "You want a guy, just like the guy, that married dear old Mom."

"Lare!" Tim says in mock reproval.

I would like to go farther in this aging American male's journey into learning to love. But instead I bounce my daughter on air at arms' length. "You must learn to amuse yourself, Molly my dear. That is the secret of getting through life."

# August 31    *Love And Laughter*

Strange, different, almost weird—those words I first think of to describe the staccato squeaks coming from the master bedroom at 7:12 this morning. I bolt from the word processor and scoot in to find what goes. Tim and Molly are facing each other at the end of a feeding.

"Whazzat!" Timarie exhales with an amazed, strangled laugh.

It elicits the same weird staccato squeaks. From Molly! She's laughing! Out loud! Molly has joined the human race...the queer genus and species that, so far as we know, is the only one that laughs...the only one that finds humor in life. I suppose when you're neither a god nor a stone, and you know it, you've got to laugh...if you don't cry.

A milestone day for Molly. But now I'm beginning to believe every one is. For at least 20 years now I've heard it said—mostly by men, I admit—that babies are little more than vegetables for the first three months, devoid of personality, occupied with eating, sleeping, evacuating, nothing more. Mothers know better. So do I now.

Or could Molly just be different? Incredibly gifted or advanced? Wouldn't it be pretty to think so. But I caution other parents as I caution myself now. Start thinking that way and you set yourself up for a fall even as you put the first chains—invisible though they be—on your child.

Molly has received a great amount of love and attention and encouragement from us; it only serves to nourish what is already there and rapidly developing. Yes, she is exceptional. So is every individual life lived—however briefly—exceptional, I'm coming to believe in my heart as well as my head.

## September 1     *Ending The Endless Summer*

How ironic the pun! That the experiment should close on this Monday traditionally celebrated by working men and women. Paradoxically, the first labor day featured much pain and great joy; this one is free of physical pain but not without sadness. Tim and I know as we rise and dress Molly for our holiday outing that a time is ending, a span in our lives together has been crossed, not to be recrossed.

We kill the morning in snacking and play...passing Molly back and forth on the living room rug to more than the usual silliness and baby-talk. In the afternoon it's off to the municipal pier. At the Pacific Ocean's eastern edge seems an appropriate place to close the circle.

The day is not so warm that Molly doesn't feel the chill as we push her stroller four lengths of the half-mile-plus-long, recently rebuilt pier, stopping to look in the fishermen's pails at their appetite-killing catch of small tomcod... and a couple of tasty bar perch that might dress out at three bites each. But everyone's content. Including Molly and Me. And Timarie makes three.

At The End—the appropriately named cafe at the pier's end—I buy two orders of home fries for Timarie and me. Delicious! As good as or better than the local touts claim.

We walk back toward town, weaving our way through human waves of all ages, colors, nationalities, and mixes of the three, their several languages briefly blending and contending in obedience to the Doppler effect, all the strollers in controlled festive moods under an afternoon semi-tropic sky. It feels comforting for the moment to be not alone, but a neutron in a not unfamiliar social nucleus.

Tim stops us halfway at the ladies' restroom for a pit stop. I edge to the western side of the pier so Molly from her stroller seat can watch the surfers in their black skins angle in the curl of the about-to-break combers. Magic. I regret for the first time that I never surfed...seriously, with a board. The sun, toward going down, backlights the slim young boys and more muscled young men out of all meaning the moment deserves. They become a visual oxymoron...a frieze of movement.

Does Molly see that? What does she see? Will Molly one day, living not three miles from breakers bragged about world wide, catch and ride them herself? Do what I never did and become a bronzed maiden of the sea? And a surfing champion while she's at it?

I feel a hand laid on mine, which rests on the raw wood of the guard rail. Slowly I bend my head, expecting to see Tim. Instead it's a crone's face. A woman maybe in her late fifties with stringy semi-red hair, weeks overdue from a proper dyeing, and a pasty, wide, sensual face—a face by Hogarth...but softened with love. "That's nice! That's nice!" the woman says to me as she pats.

It takes me too many seconds to realize what she means. She's pleased to see a man my age caring for a baby, alone. I don't have the heart to tell her we're not two generations of orphans...that my wife, who is of the bridging generation, will return shortly...though she should not be dismayed by, or critical of, her youngish looks....

The woman has already turned away and waddled off toward The End. Belatedly, I spin the stroller toward her, wanting to explain.

I'm still looking southwest, into the low marine stratus moving in, when Timarie sneaks up on me from behind. "What you doing, sailor?"

"Just looking...to sea, ma'am."

"Want a date?"

"If you'll let me take my daughter along."

"Yeah, OK, she's cute...ever been to Neptune's Locker?"

"Not that I know of...it's off-limits to sailors, I think."

"Well, do you dare?"

"Always. So long as it's safe."

"You're in luck, sailor...it's only 200 feet from the very spots we stand on."

A surprise to me, Neptune's Locker turns out not to be packed, and we manage to find two newly vacated stools at the westward viewing window, next to the Pac-Man machine. We've parked the stroller outside on the pier and I hold Molly while Timarie orders two beers and then returns with them, served in the house's own mugs—small canning jars with handles.

"Happy days!" Timarie raises her jar in toast.

"Happy days," I echo with less enthusiasm.

"Why don't you play some music? Here, I'll take Molly."

I hand Molly over, fish a quarter out of my pocket and take the familiar few steps to the juke box. It offers 180 selections, but most are rock songs I don't know by groups I've never heard of. Of the few selections

I do recognize, I punch "Classical Gas," "The Greatest Love" and, appropriately, the Beach Boys' "Surfin' USA."

By the time I reseat myself, Mason Williams is plucking his guitar.

"Nice choice," Timarie says.

"Thank you," I respond, though I'm looking west to where the clouds are thickening and will probably mar our sunset.

"Checking the weather?"

"Yeah." I smile sheepishly. Timarie is referring to a habit of mine at emotional times of surveying the sky, reverting to work habits of three decades back, when I put in four years plus in the Air Force's Air Weather Service. She recognizes the dodge. She knows I'm coming down from my great summer high and that a new semester will begin with shocking abruptness tomorrow. The intimate life the three of us have shared will change, by necessity be less intimate.

"I've got a present for you."

"You do?"

"Yes." She reaches into Molly's lavender diaperbag and extracts a porcelain picture frame decorated with diminuitive lavender flowers. "Here. It's for your desk, so you can have your favorite picture of your favorite daughter at school."

In the frame is one of the several-dozen snapshots Tim's had blown up to five-by-seven size—it's the one I call "La Baigneuse." Molly's in her yellow plastic bathtub looking out at the camera, her mouth a perfect "O" and her blue eyes just as round. Her dampened hair spirals into dark red curls atop a little, plumping body that's a color cross between pink and peach.

Thoughtful. It may be the best present I ever received.

Neptune's friendly habitues—mostly young beachy people—soon make contact with the unlikely family in their midst. Molly's the main attraction, but Timarie, always gregarious, is now Ms. Mixer with her baby to proudly show the world—or at least any one who will answer her or Molly's smile. I hang back and let the curious do their sleuthing as to where I fit in the picture. Some are more direct than others and flat out ask me, "Are you the father?" Their incredulity—or is it wonder?—passes quickly enough. As a lot they're tolerant—a trait I find generally shared by Californians who live on the littoral.

"Are you going to have any more?"

The question comes from my blindside...from a stocky, open-faced beach-blonded woman in her mid-twenties. It's one Timarie and I have been asked a few times before, though we know many others would like to ask but don't want to appear rude.

"Yes, at least one more... in a couple of years," I respond, though the question was apparently meant for Tim.

The young woman flashes me one of those "sez-you, Methuselah" looks, then gives up her skepticism. "Really? You want a boy or a girl?"

"We haven't settled on a sex yet," I say, realizing as I hear the words how arrogant they sound. "We'll take anything we get," I lamely amend.

"Got the names picked out?" About a half-dozen beer-sipping patrons have stopped crunching their Cheetos and have cocked an ear to hear.

"Yes," I say, deciding to anticipate a couple of coming questions. "If it's a boy it will be Franz Lawrence. The Franz is after a mutual friend we have in Germany; Lawrence is my wife's surname, which she continues to use, much to the confusion of banks and insurance companies; Lawrence was also my father's first name. If it's a girl, she'll be Madeline Jeannette—Madeline just because we both like it, and Jeannette because it was my mother's name."

The answer is decisive. Talk stops and more patrons are going than coming now, because the sun's well down. We should be going, too. It's dinner time and beyond. But preferring to make it another marathon Labor Day, we decide to drive six miles to the Harbor House, a world-class hamburger joint we both like. Molly can always nurse nestled among the layers of blouse and sweater and blanket.

We get a back patio seat under the night stars. Our waitress, a pleasant and very young woman, is quite taken with the baby and asks Timarie her name.

"Molly."

"That's a nice name! After Molly Ringwald?"

"No, Molly Bloom," I intrude, not really kidding. I don't know much about the actress; but Joyce's woman is... well... if not the perfect role model, at least she is much woman.

"She looks Irish," the waitress says as she brings our burgers and fries.

"She is," Timarie confirms, proudly, stretching things. Tim's only half Irish. My mother was also half Irish and gave Molly her red hair. So, I guess Molly has every right to look Irish. Whatever, she is a lot cuter than most bugs' ears. And active, active, active—mostly with her hands. I watch her use them to touch her ears, her mouth, her hair, as I've watched them finger Tim's nursing bra straps when nursing, diapers and rompers when she's being dressed, medication containers when she gets her bum salved—most everything in reach. Handy hands. Yes, constant exploration with those handy hands has become her *modus operandi*. She is beginning to manipulate her world.

But not right now. Molly starts a royal fuss, punctuated with hunger cries. Tim lifts her sweatshirt, opens a bra cup, and "plugs her in," as she likes to put it. Not for long. At 9:16 p.m. the sucking stops. Molly passes out. Time to head home. My summer with Molly is over.

# September 2     *The Morning After*

I'm up early and at the Kaypro because I can't let things end with last night. I've still got a couple of hours before I'm off to meet my Advanced Magazine Article Writing class for the first time, and I want to use some of those minutes to try some kind of wrap-up.

Did I accomplish what I set out to do? Not by any stretch of the imagination. The novel I was going to revise lies untouched. The course plan for "Journalism as Literature" I intended to revise and revitalize remains its old tired self. The lawn has not been reseeded, the driveway has not been resurfaced, my writing room has not been repainted.

And yet I think I've just lived the most productive summer of my life. My soul is nourished. My mind thinks younger than in the spring. I hope and like to believe that Molly has benefited, too. That through our closeness, through the strokes and whispers and rhymes and songs and games and much touching, I have given her something of value. Not something she'll remember, but something that may help mold her.

And I have this journal. Friends ask me what I intend to do with it. Get it published, of course. What a question to ask a writer! Maybe I'll publish it myself. And if an unkind fate should yank me out of life before I get it done? Well, there will always be this manuscript copy for Molly to read someday.

I really want to stay home with Molly this day, and for many more tomorrows after that. I'm even tempted to ask the dean if I can't have the next academic year off, and have my checks mailed to my home on the first of the month. Kind of an informal sabbatical, on which I would finally write that promised textbook on "How to Publish the Student Magazine." Or maybe I could swing a grant to study "Possible Innate Prejudices as Manifest in the Selective Punishment of the Candlestickmaker from a Random Sample of 100 Babies Playing with 'Three Men in a Tub.'"

Well, I doubt that would fly either. Fisher Price might be up to underwriting the research, but I don't think my dean would approve.

So now I hit the last keys and get ready to take Molly to her first regular babysitter. Painful thought, that.

Still, if providence is kind, there will be other summers for us to share. In any case, she will one day know that her first summer on earth was for me, of the the 53 I've been around, by far the best.

## May 13, 1987     *Anniversary Postscript*

I write this postscript on a city park table, where Tim and I have brought Molly to celebrate her first birthday. Our girl is too excited to eat much tuna salad, which doesn't prevent Tim and me from devouring our tuna-on-whole-wheat sandwiches, the Hawaiian-thick potato chips, and a chill bottle of Napa Valley Riesling. The late afternoon is uncharacteristically gray and muggy, but we don't mind. We are here to feed the ducks...the ducks and mallards and mudhens and all manner of our web-footed friends who gulp our proferred popcorn. Well, Molly doesn't quite feed them...but she points at all the birds that come and go; she points at everything. So much so that I have come to call her "The Pointer."

Molly is a sturdy 19 pounds and eight ounces now, still blue-eyed, her hair lustrous strands of rich champagne that are forming four little vertical sausage curls above her neck's nape. She has eight front teeth which she bares in her frequent smiles.

For a month now she's been walking that charming semi-stumble of the toddler, getting into everything not locked up or hidden. She can say "Da Da" and "Kurt" and "Mama," "Hi" and "bye-bye" and "night-night," and most recently "zat" (as in "what's that?"), usually in the company of an extended index finger, and "look"—also used in connection with a finger pointing at something.

Timarie has blossomed further into the rapt, loving supermother destiny decreed. Molly is her joy daily felt. "What would we do without that girl?" she asks me often, happy on the verge of fear and tears.

I dread the answer. Neither can I imagine life without her...without them. I have found more happiness than I deserve from a life rather recklessly lived.

Even though the aches and pains are inexorably slowing and stiffening me, I can still crouch down beside Molly, sight along her finger toward the horizon, which is smaller and brighter now, to see if she has found what I've always looked for. I think again. Maybe The Pointer is what I should have been looking for all along.

Book Design
and Illustrations
By Elin Waite

The Text Is
11 on 13 Point
Goudy Old Style

Production by Dynacomp
Printed on Acid-Free Paper in the
United States of America